THE Lincoln DEL COOKBOOK

THE Lincoln DEL COOKBOOK

BEST-LOVED Recipes

from the legendary bakery and deli

WENDI ZELKIN ROSENSTEIN

AND KIT NAYLOR

Foreword by
THOMAS L. FRIEDMAN

MINNESOTA HISTORICAL SOCIETY PRESS

www.mnhspress.org

The Minnesota Historical Society Press is a member of the Association of American University Presses.

Manufactured in the United States of America

10 9 8 7 6 5 4 3

∞ The paper used in this publication meets the minimum requirements of the American National Standard for Information Sciences—Permanence for Printed Library Materials, ANSI Z39.48-1984.

International Standard Book Number
ISBN: 978-1-68134-061-6 (paper)

Library of Congress Cataloging-in-Publication Data
Names: Rosenstein, Wendi Zelkin, 1962- author. | Naylor, Kit, 1953- author.
Title: The Lincoln Del cookbook : best-loved recipes from the legendary bakery and deli /
    Wendi Zelkin Rosenstein and Kit Naylor ; foreword by Thomas L. Friedman.
Description: St. Paul, MN : Minnesota Historical Society Press, [2017] | Includes index.
Identifiers: LCCN 2017010961 | ISBN 9781681340616 (pbk. : alk. paper)
Subjects: LCSH: Baking. | Cooking. | Lincoln Del Restaurant. | LCGFT: Cookbooks.
Classification: LCC TX765 .R738 2017 | DDC 641.81/5—dc23
LC record available at https://lccn.loc.gov/2017010961

Unless otherwise noted, all images are from the Berenberg family's collection.

Decorative doilies by Aleksey Fefelov.

WITH LOVE AND AFFECTION

this book is dedicated to the memory

of Baubie Tess and Zadie Moishe Berenberg,

who filled my life with stability, unconditional love,

and the strong sense of family and Jewish community

that I have carried throughout my life and have

shared with my beloved children, Brett and Matthew.

— W Z R —

A Jewish cookbook can be almost considered a history book . . . a history of 5700 years of happiness and sorrow. Jewish cooking, since the kettles of the Hebrews have simmered in every country of the world . . . is thoroughly international in flavor.

PAUL GROSSINGER, *The Art of Jewish Cooking*

It seems to me that our three basic needs, for food and security and love, are so mixed and mingled and entwined that we cannot straightly think of one without the others. So it happens that when I write of hunger, I am really writing about love and the hunger for it, and warmth and the love of it and the hunger for it . . . and then the warmth and richness and fine reality of hunger satisfied . . . and it is all one.

M. F. K. FISHER, *The Art of Eating*

CONTENTS

FOREWORD

Matzo Balls and Memories

IF THE JEWISH COMMUNITY of Minnesota had a beating heart—a holy of holies of food, conversation, and camaraderie—it was not a synagogue or the Jewish Community Center. It was the Lincoln Delicatessen, mostly just known as "The Del."

Just saying those two words brings back a flood of memories to my mind—and stomach. My mother, Margaret, worked as a bookkeeper at the Del in the basement on Lake Street to put my sister Jane through Bryn Mawr College. Jane worked at the Del on Highway 12 as a waitress during her school breaks, and as a little boy I used to play on the baker's wooden tables, sometimes braiding challahs. Owners Morrie and Tess Berenberg were dear friends of my parents, and I knew them my whole life. Morrie held court at the Lake Street Del at a central table in the dining room every afternoon and evening, entertaining customers while keeping an eye on the deli counter and the staff.

I love how the authors of this book, Wendi Zelkin Rosenstein and Kit Naylor, describe the scene: "For Jewish and non-Jewish customers alike, it was the Minneapolis version of *Cheers*, except that at the Del everybody really *did* know your name. . . . It was the place for everyone to meet after school or before a movie, to tailgate before a bus ride to a sports event, to get engaged, or to celebrate life after a funeral. From graduations to business meetings, the Lincoln Del remains a touchstone for people who grew up in Minneapolis and St. Louis Park."

It certainly was for our family. What was the Del's secret recipe? Why is it so fondly etched in the memories of so many of us who grew up in Minneapolis in the 1950s, 1960s, and 1970s? Was it just the food? Of course not. The Del "sold" something so much more compelling that kept its customers constantly coming back, and which is increasingly rare these days. It wasn't knishes—*it was community*. Anybody could learn how to make knishes and sell them. But what I, and so many others, actually remember most was the community and bonding that we engaged in at the Del. The times we squeezed into a booth with family, friends, or a first date and forged bonds that hold to this day.

My friend the British environmentalist Tom Burke likes to say that "it's the doing we do together that matters most." We are hardwired from our days as hunter-gatherers to do things together. And I am convinced that when we do, some hormone is released by our brains that fosters a feeling of warmth. The Del had that effect on many of us because it was a place where we did things together. And if you hopped from booth to booth you could be together with so many others doing things together, and together it all wove this warm tapestry of community. The knishes just made it extra special.

I confess that living in Washington, DC, I have no such place to go where you know lots of people and people call you by your first name, where the owner greets you, as Morrie would, with the politically incorrect, "Hey, Jew, come sit down," and where you can hop from table to table and shake hands, gossip, and have a good laugh with so many other customers. The delicatessens here only sell knishes, not community. They offer matzo balls, but without memories. That is why whenever I eat at one of them, no matter how much I eat, I always leave hungry. My stomach is full, but my soul is empty. Nobody ever left the Del hungry. It filled body and soul.

So my hat is off to Wendi and Kit for understanding that to tell the history of the Del, which they have done so remarkably, you have to weave together its recipes for cooking memories and matzo balls, knishes and community, because the Del had a unique way of making both—and I am not sure which I miss most.

Thomas L. Friedman
Bethesda, Maryland (but always still from Minnesota)

THE Lincoln DEL COOKBOOK

This book celebrates the couple who started it all,
Frima Leah (Fanny) and Frank Berenberg

The Family Business

If you have bread and butter, you have good luck.
Host broit mit puter iz der mazel a gutter.
YIDDISH PROVERB

At home I serve the kind of food I know the story behind.
MICHAEL POLLAN

MORRIE (MOISHE) BERENBERG walked in the back door of Lincoln Del East in St. Louis Park, Minnesota. The aroma of fresh bread greeted him from the moment he opened his car door and as he strolled to the large-windowed steel delivery door. He glanced at the yellow-tiled, cavernous but bright bakery, warm with heat from the two giant rotating ovens that operated twenty-four hours a day, seven days a week. The white-clad bakers were sliding bread and bagels into the ovens, and pastry chefs and cake decorators stood at the long butcher-block tables, working alongside tall carts of freshly baked goods to be delivered to all three Lincoln Del locations. Some of the employees had just started their early-morning shifts; some waved good-bye as they ascended the back basement stairs after finishing their overnight shifts.

Morrie continued down the back hallway, grabbing a warm, just-baked egg bagel off the tall cooling rack, taking a bite and grabbing a piece of bologna or salami left on the deli slicer. He always had a smile as he greeted his staff. He continued past the deli cases, glanced at the front door to confirm that there was someone at the register, noted the oil painting of his parents, Frank and Fanny Berenberg, hanging behind it, counted the customers waiting for their deli and bakery orders, made sure the frozen cases were full of product, then settled into his usual table and ordered a cup of coffee, black. Chef Bill gave him a raspy hello from the open kitchen behind the front line of waitresses filling silver bowls of pickled beets and half-dill pickles that would soon sit at every table—the "relish trays" that regular customer Barb Pratt still thinks of as the Jewish version of Holy Communion.

Morrie liked to hold court at one of the long tables in the back half of the restaurant, across from the open kitchen, facing the hostess stand so he could see his customers come and go. Even into his seventies, Morrie, along with his wife, Tess, often worked twelve-hour days. Tess checked everything that came out of the kitchen, and if it wasn't right, she'd send it back. When she wasn't expediting the kitchen orders, Tess sat across from Morrie, watching that the plates got picked up immediately and went to the right tables. Morrie could monitor the front as people paid for their purchases, see who bought from the bakery and deli, and glance to the left as folks hung their coats, placed a call on the pay phone, or turned to walk down the stairs to the restrooms, prep kitchen, or locked office. It was the perfect division of labor.

Friends often hurried over for a handshake and a wisecrack. Every morning, in response to Morrie's "Where ya been? Are you hungry? Sit down, I wanna ask you something," customers took him up on a cup of coffee and a nosh. There was always a story to tell, a relative to check up on, the well-being of a son or daughter in college to inquire about, or the next trip to Arizona or the "fat farm" in California to plan. Morrie spent hours at each location, walking through the bakery and deli, touching base with employees as well as friends coming and going all day.

One of those coffee and nosh discussions took place in 1973 between Morrie and a young Thomas Friedman, well before the start of his successful journalism career. The families were close: Friedman's mother, Margaret, worked as the Del's bookkeeper, and his father, Harold "Iggy," had worked with Morrie's best friend, Jake Garber. Friedman's father had just died, and Thomas, a freshman at Brandeis University, was home for the funeral, unsure of his immediate future. Morrie told him to go back to Boston, to finish college, and not to worry about his tuition. Morrie gathered his closest friends, and they all pitched in. Though Morrie had never

Lincoln Del Breakfast Menu

THE Lincoln DEL

Lincoln Del East
4100 Minnetonka Blvd., St. Louis Park, MN

Lincoln Del South
4401 West 80th St., Bloomington, MN

Fresh Bakery & Cereal

Bagel 1.55
Egg bagel, water bagel, raisin bagel
or onion bagel

Toast with Butter and Jam 1.40
White (egg pan), pumpernickel, light rye,
onion rye, caraway rye, whole wheat,
Lincoln whole wheat, kaiser roll

Oven-Fresh Danish Roll, butter 1.95

Fresh Doughnut 1.35

Toasted English Muffin
Butter and jam

Dry Cereal with Half & Half 1.45
With bananas and Half & Half 2.65
. . . . 3.25

Cooked Oatmeal with Half & Half
With bananas and Half & Half 2.95
With walnuts, white raisins, brown . . . 3.45
sugar and Half & Half
(Add 50¢ for bananas) 4.35

Breakfast Specialties

Breakfast Taco
Eggs scrambled with spinach, jalapeno jack cheese
in softshell taco. Mango salsa on the side.
Shoestring potatoes.
. . . . 9.65

Pancakes
With butter and maple syrup 4.65

Blueberry Pancakes
With butter and maple syrup 4.95

Egg Fluffs (French Toast)
With butter and maple syrup 6.35

Two Cheese Blintzes 7.55
Three Cheese Blintzes 10.45
A cheese mixture in a thin crepe
served with two of the following:
sour cream, strawberry jam, blueberry
compote, or cherry compote

Beverages

Beverages
Coffee or Decaffeinated Coffee 1.65
Pot of Tea or Pot of Decaffeinated Tea
Milk, Chocolate Milk or Hot Chocolate

Pop (Fountain) 1.65

Made Famous at the Del

Hoppel Poppel Eggs
Scrambled with frankfurters and onions . . 9.95

Scrambled Eggs,
Lox and Onions 12.95

Corned Beef Hash with one egg 10.25
Orders above served with choice of
bagel or toast

Five Potato Pancakes
With sour cream or apple sauce 8.45

Original Omelettes

We use farm-fresh eggs and pure creamery
butter. Omelettes are served with
choice of toast or bagel

Cheese Omelette 7.25
Corned Beef and Cheese 9.65
Pastrami and Cheese 9.65
Salami and Cheese 9.65
Bologna and Cheese 9.65
Tongue and Cheese 9.65
Chicken Livers and Cheese 9.85
Bacon and Cheese 9.95
Sausage and Cheese 9.65
Ham and Cheese 9.65
Canadian Bacon and Cheese 9.65
Spanish Omelette 9.65
Plain Omelette (no cheese) 8.95
. . . . 6.75
Add to Omelettes: Mushrooms 1.45 extra
Green Peppers 1.15 extra
Substitute EggStro'dnaire, add 1.00

Cheese Choices: American, Swiss, Cheddar
Hot pepper or Muenster

Wake Up Eggs

Two Eggs with toast or bagel 3.95

Corned Beef or Pastrami and Eggs . . 9.75
With toast or bagel

Salami or Bologna and Eggs 9.35
With toast or bagel

Western Omelette 8.95
(Pancake style) corned beef, green peppers
and onions with toast or bagel

Matzo and Eggs scrambled style 8.95

*All Egg Items Can Be Prepared with EggStro'dnaire
including Egg Fluffs (French Toast). Add 1.00*

Side Orders

Two Eggs 2.75
One Egg 1.95
Bacon or Sausage 3.35
Ham 3.35
Canadian Bacon 3.55
Fried Salami or Bologna 3.55
Hash Brown Potatoes 3.85
Cream Cheese 90
Smoked Salmon (lox) 10.45
Potato Pancakes
With sour cream or apple sauce 4.95

Fruits and Juices

Orange Juice fresh-squeezed 2.95
Grapefruit Juice 2.15
Apple Juice 2.15
Tomato Juice 2.15
1/2 Grapefruit in season 2.95
1/2 Cantaloupe in season 2.95
Delicious Baked Apple in season 3.50
Bananas with Half & Half 2.95
Small Dish Mixed Fresh Fruit
(In light sugar syrup) 2.95

These Items are EXCLUSIVE to the Lincoln Dels
Cigar and pipe smoking allowed
in the bar only.

graduated from high school, he was a firm believer in higher education and the promise of a strong career. He saw Friedman's intelligence and potential. And, indeed, Friedman's choice of schools was the start of a family legacy: Morrie's first granddaughter, Wendi, graduated from Brandeis in 1984, and his twin great-grandsons, who are named in his memory, are members of the Brandeis class of 2018. Yet, despite his fervent belief in higher education, Morrie hated to see his girls leave home for any reason. He would look at Wendi and say, "What's wrong with the U?" (referring to the nearby University of Minnesota). "Boston is too far."

Morrie's conversation with Thomas Friedman was just one example of many similar discussions held at a table at the Lincoln Del. Lives were planned, disputes settled, deals made, family events celebrated, and friendships nurtured. All over a great nosh and a cup of coffee. 🖤

Jan 1-1982

Special Breakfast Treats

Fruits and Juices

SCRAMBLED EGGS
Smoked Salmon (Lox) and Onions
5.25 ✓

CHEESE OMELETTE
3.85 ✓

CORNED BEEF HASH
5.50 ✓
with 1 Egg, Fried or Poached
6.00 ✓

Above Orders Include Toast - Bagel or Kaiser Roll

ORANGE JUICE (Freshly Squeezed) 1.15
Large Glass 1.60
GRAPEFRUIT JUICE .... .85
Large Glass 1.35
TOMATO JUICE .... .85
Large Glass 1.35
½ GRAPEFRUIT (In Season) ....
CANTALOUPE (In Season) ....
DELICIOUS BAKED APPLE (In Season) .
YOUR CHOICE OF FRUITS:
Prunes, Peaches, Fruit Cocktail ... 1.35
BANANAS and HALF & HALF 1.35

Beverages

COFFEE .... .55
DECAFFEINATED COFFEE .... .55
POT OF TEA .... .55
MILK .... .65
CHOCOLATE MILK .... .65
HOT CHOCOLATE .... .75

PANCAKES
Butter and Maple Syrup
2.40 ✓

BLUEBERRY PANCAKES
Thin, Tasty Treats Served with Butter and Extra Blueberries
3.15 ✓

FRENCH EGG FLUFFS
(French Toast)
Served with Butter and Maple Syrup
3.25 ✓

Toast-Pastries-Cereals

BAGEL or KAISER ROLL, Butter/Jam .... .95
TOAST, Butter and Jam .... .80
HEALTH WHOLE WHEAT TOAST .... .80
OVEN FRESH DANISH ROLL, Butter/Jam .... .75
TOASTED ENGLISH MUFFIN, Butter/Jam .... .90
CINNAMON TOAST .... .80
DRY or COOKED CEREAL with Half & Half 1.35
DRY CEREAL with Bananas 1.75

Side Orders

SIDE OF TWO EGGS .... 1.40 ✓
SIDE OF ONE EGG .... .90 ✓
SIDE OF BACON or SAUSAGE .... 1.50 ✓
SIDE OF HAM .... 1.75 ✓
SIDE OF CANADIAN BACON .... 1.65 ✓
SIDE OF FRIED SALAMI or BOLOGNA .... 1.55 ✓
SIDE OF HASH BROWN POTATOES .... 1.85 ✓
SIDE OF CREAM CHEESE .... .50 ✓
SIDE OF SMOKED FISH .... 3.95 ✓
SIDE OF SMOKED SALMON (Lox 2 oz.) ...... 2.65 ✓
— All Prices Subject to Minnesota State Sales Tax —

Omelettes

WE USE FARM FRESH EGGS IN PURE CREAMERY BUTTER
CHEESE OMELETTE .... 3.85 ✓
CORNED BEEF and CHEESE .... 5.45 ✓
PASTRAMI and CHEESE .... 5.45 ✓
SALAMI and CHEESE .... 5.10 ✓
BOLOGNA and CHEESE .... 5.10 ✓
TONGUE and CHEESE .... 5.15 ✓
CHICKEN LIVERS and CHEESE .... 5.15 ✓
BACON and CHEESE .... 5.15 ✓
HAM and CHEESE .... 5.15 ✓
CANADIAN BACON and CHEESE .... 5.15 ✓
JELLY and CHEESE .... 3.95 ✓
Choice of Toast, Bagel or Kaiser Roll Included with Above Omelettes
ABOVE OMELETTES WITH   GREEN PEPPERS .75 Extra
MUSHROOMS .95 Extra   OMELETTES WITHOUT CHEESE .40 Less
ONIONS .50 Extra

Eggs

TWO EGGS .... 1.95 ✓
CORNED BEEF or PASTRAMI and EGGS ...... 4.65 ✓
SALAMI or BOLOGNA and EGGS 3.95
Choice of Toast, Bagel or Kaiser Roll Included in Above Egg Orders
MATZO and EGGS .... 3.50 ✓

GOOD MORNING
breakfast is now being served.

A Jewish Family in Minneapolis

Love is sweet, but it's good with bread.
Di libe iz zis nor ziiz gut mit broit.
YIDDISH PROVERB

Troubles with soup is easier than troubles without soup.
Tsores mit yoykh iz grinder vi tsores on yoykh.
YIDDISH PROVERB

WHEN HE EMIGRATED from Romania in 1897 as part of a wave of Yiddish-speaking Jews, twenty thousand of whom ended up in Minnesota between 1882 and 1924, Frank Berenberg brought with him a treasure more precious than diamonds: the sour starter that ensured his family's success for the next three generations. "Sour," a "secret" ingredient of all bakeries, is a living organism. It has to be fed with flour every day or it dies. A skilled baker, Frank understood the value of his thousand-year-old sour, and he managed to keep it alive all the way across the Atlantic.

Frank was just a teenager, only fifteen or so, and he arrived alone. Relatives think he must have worked on the ship to pay for his passage. Frank landed in New York and eventually made his way to Chicago—the usual east-to-west immigration pattern—and then came to Minnesota. He initially went to Virginia, Minnesota, because somebody told him that Virginia was the capital of the state. Finding that he'd been completely misinformed, he moved instead to Minneapolis.

Frank Berenberg—in partnership with the Malinsky family—established the Northside Bakery in 1930 in North Minneapolis. Along with the People's Bakery, they comprised a true community of bakers, each helping the other when supplies ran low, when a delivery needed to be covered, when an extra oven was needed to fill an order. The unspoken rule was that they helped each other on a handshake. Even in 2013, years after the first deal was made between the Malinskys and the Berenbergs, Bookie Malinsky called Frank Berenberg's grandson, Danny Berenberg, to get the phone number for the head baker, Roger Malikowski, to ask him to make Bookie's favorite, blueberry muffins.

The story goes that Frank was so enamored of America's freedoms, and of "Honest Abe" Lincoln in particular, that he named his first son Abraham and his business Lincoln. In 1933, Frank incorporated the Lincoln Bakery, opening on Lyndale Avenue in North Minneapolis and bringing sons Abraham (known as Robert, or "Boonie"), Irving ("Izzy"), and Moishe ("Morris" or "Morrie") and daughters Ann, Agnes, and Gloria into the business in about 1935.

Frank sold the Lincoln Bakery/Lincoln Bakery Company to his sons in 1946, a dark time for the Jewish community. As the baking company evolved into the Lincoln Del Bakery, Restaurants and Delicatessens (known collectively as "the Lincoln Del") in the 1950s, '60s, and '70s, Twin Cities Jewish life was transforming. Opening midway between the virulent anti-Semitism of the 1930s and '40s and the assimilation of the late '60s,

Lincoln Bakery, North Minneapolis, circa 1930s. Frank Berenberg is standing in the middle.

the original Del bridged the gap between old and new cultures. The immigrant families of Minnesota were accustomed to empty pantries. They appreciated the memories the Del's food brought them in a simple piece of rye bread or a slice of kosher salami. At the Del, grandparents could share with their American-born grandchildren a nosh that tasted just like the bread they ate in the "old country."

It's hard to imagine now, but Minneapolis was once proclaimed "the capital of anti-Semitism in the United States." In a 1946 essay, "Minneapolis: The Curious Twin," published in *Common Ground*, Carey McWilliams declared, "In almost every walk of life, an 'iron curtain' separates Jews from non-Jews in Minneapolis."

McWilliams argued that discrimination was much more pronounced in Minneapolis than in its easterly twin, St. Paul. No major industries or businesses would hire Jewish men. Jews were banned from membership in private country clubs and excluded from such organizations as Lions and Kiwanis Clubs, Rotary, the Toastmasters, even the Minneapolis chapter of the American Automobile Association. Denied access to Minneapolis medical facilities and prohibited from admitting patients unless arranging to do so through a non-Jewish doctor, Jewish physicians built their own hospital, Mount Sinai. Restrictive neighborhoods—Edina, for example—barred Jews and other minorities from buying property or renting housing. Summer resorts on Lake Minnetonka catered to "Gentiles only."

From 1921 until he retired in 1963, Albert J. Minda served as rabbi of Temple Israel, the first Jewish congregation in Minneapolis, established in 1879. He joined clergy at neighboring churches to found the Minneapolis Urban League and the Minneapolis chapter of the National Conference of Christians and Jews. Rabbi Minda became a regular speaker at civic groups, service clubs, labor organizations, and local churches, emphasizing common ties of fellowship and brotherhood.

By 1948, Minneapolis mayor Hubert Humphrey appointed a task force that confirmed allegations of anti-Semitism and discrimination against other minorities. That task force became permanent as the Mayor's Council on Human Relations and eventually passed ordinances outlawing anti-Semitic and racist policies in housing and employment. Humphrey was among many politicians who were regulars at the Del. Morrie Berenberg was proud to introduce Humphrey to his grandchildren, telling them that public service was an important career and that public servants were very helpful to the Jewish community.

It's hard to know which came first: whether with assimilation, Jewish food became more palatable to midwestern tastes, or whether bakeries like the Del introduced non-Jews to a culture known for its nosh. In any case, barriers relaxed after World War II, and the Jewish population moved west to the suburbs, most notably St. Louis Park, where Jews could freely buy homes and open businesses. A bakery with a historic sour behind it would flourish in this new neighborhood.

During the early days of the Lincoln Del, particularly in the St. Louis Park location (the "Old Joint"), Jewish patrons felt welcomed and at home. Morrie's granddaughter Wendi remembers working at the counter, serving many elderly Jewish customers who placed the same daily orders, often simply pointing to what they wanted in the bakery case, commenting in Yiddish then asking in English, "How's your Baubie and Zadie?"

The Del's baked goods were of the highest-quality ingredients and freshly made around the clock. Recipes began not only in the Russian and Romanian Berenberg family kitchens but also in the German and Polish farmhouses where Tess Berenberg's family originated.

Theresa Clara Schmidt Berenberg ("Baubie Tess") wasn't born Jewish; she was originally Lutheran, and she grew up on a farm in Hutchinson, Minnesota, the only girl with five brothers. Morrie met her when she worked at Abe's Delicatessen in North Minneapolis and he delivered their bread orders. Morrie had an eye for the ladies, and Tess was blonde and blue-eyed, a good-looking gal. He would have his best friend, Jake Garber, pick him up in the morning after his midnight baking shift and drive him over to see Tess. Later, in 1938, when Morrie and Tess were twenty and twenty-one, Garber drove them to Milbank, South Dakota, to get married by a justice of the peace. Tess's in-laws, Frank and Fanny Berenberg, took to her right away because they saw that she was a straight talker and a hard worker. Tess eventually converted to Judaism.

By 1951, the Lincoln Bakery operated two retail locations in Minneapolis.

LINCOLN DEL *Lexicon*

Found in a Lincoln Del Employee Guidelines notebook from the early 1960s.

→ *The following is a glossary of Jewish words that when memorized and sprinkled into your conversation will impress your Jewish customers! (Notice the uniquely Jewish syntax of that last sentence!)*

1. GEFILTE FISH . . . pronounced ge-fill-the . . . rhymes with Attila dish. From the German: "stuffed fish." Fish cakes or balls or loaves of various fishes which are chopped or ground and mixed with eggs, salt, and lots of onions and pepper (and sometimes sugar). VERY traditional food usually served with red horseradish. Definitely an acquired taste!

2. ROSH HASHANAH . . . rawsh-ha-shaw-neh . . . rhymes with "cautious fauna." The Jewish New Year, one of the holiest days in the Jewish calendar.

3. YOM KIPPUR . . . pronounced yum-kip-per to rhyme with "hum dipper" . . . means "Day of Atonement," the holiest day of the Jewish calendar . . . total fast . . . no food or drink from sundown to sundown but some break the fast early. Day of group confession where Jews ask forgiveness from other people.

4. SHOFAR . . . pronounced show-fer to rhyme with "toe fir" . . . a ram's horn which has been made into a wind instrument that when blown gives off a very piercing sound . . . blown in synagogues to alert people to their weaknesses . . . Yom Kippur ends with the blowing of the shofar, sometimes with as many as six of them at the same time.

5. CHALLAH . . . pronounced HAL-leh, with the rattling kh . . . rhymes with "doll-a." On Rosh Hashanah and Yom Kippur the challah is round to symbolize the world. It's called either a turban challah or KITKA which rhymes with "sit-pa." To make it sweeter for the holidays we bake it with raisins.

6. SHUL . . . which rhymes with "fuel" is Yiddish for synagogue.

7. BLINTZ . . . which rhymes with "chintz." From Ukrainian "pancake" . . . it's a pancake, rolled around a filling, most often cottage cheese. These wonderful delicacies are smothered under thick sour cream. Jet-set Jews have taken to smothering blintzes with honey or jam instead of sour cream. There is no accounting for tastes!

8. MANDEL BREAD . . . rhymes with "fondle dead." The Jewish response to biscotti . . . a twice-baked "cookie" made with almonds (mandel).

9. KMISH BREAD . . . pronounce the "k" . . . and it rhymes with "ka-trish." A "cookie" with a soft dough filled with jam and nuts.

10. RUGALACH . . . pronounced roo-ga-lach with the rattling kh at the end. It rhymes with "ohh-la-la." Another pastry with a soft dough and filled with cinnamon, nuts, jam, etc. Ask Jewish people about rugalach and they'll maintain that their mother or grandmother made the best! *L*

The store at 2003 Plymouth Avenue was a "cold shop," where baked goods were sold but not made. At 1405 Sixth Avenue North, Olson Memorial Highway, was the wholesale bakery that supplied bread to many Minneapolis and St. Paul businesses. Cold shops were also located at Snyder Drug Stores, as well as at the famous Great Northern Market at Eighth and Hennepin in Minneapolis, which was often run by the Berenberg sisters, Agnes, Ann, and Gloria. The Olson Highway location was displaced in 1957 with the improvement of Highway 55, and the operation was moved to St. Louis Park.

The Berenberg family, now including Morrie's wife, Tess, opened their first Lincoln Del in 1957. "The Joint" or "the Old Del" was the original bakery, deli, and (later) restaurant at 4100 Minnetonka Boulevard/Lake

In 1936, bakers went on strike to demand the right to form a union. Those who chose to work during the strike sneaked to the bakery inside the bakery truck. Izzy on left, Morrie on right.

GRAND OPENING
of the
LINCOLN BAKERY

1405 Sixth Avenue No.

APRIL 27   **APRIL 27**

With a Complete Line of
BREAD, ROLLS, PASTRY
Fresh Merchandise Always

Your old friend Frank Berenberg is back and has again ventured in the Bakery Business. He will give you the same courteous treatment as of old

Be Sure to Visit Our New Bakery on Opening Day
SATURDAY, APRIL 27th
LINCOLN BAKERY CO.

HYland 4100

1405 - Sixth Avenue North

We Deliver

This advertisement celebrates the start of the Lincoln Bakery's retail business on April 27, 1935, just two days after Morrie's birthday.

Street in St. Louis Park. "Lincoln Del West," a cocktail lounge, bakery, deli, and restaurant on Highway 100 and Highway 12/Highway 394 in St. Louis Park, was originally run by Jack Zelkin, Morrie's son-in-law and the author's father. The family operated another cocktail lounge, bakery, deli, and restaurant on Highway 494 and France Avenue in Bloomington.

The Dels were always family-owned and -operated businesses. As one former employee put it, "There was always a Berenberg on the premises. If you were loyal to them, they were very generous to you." Those three Lincoln Del restaurants were all supplied from the central bakery on Lake Street.

If you had something to talk about with a family member, friend, or colleague, you'd say, "Meet me at the Del" to discuss matters over a cup of coffee and a sandwich.

Former customer Michelle Price remembers: "The Lincoln Del was one of a kind, with a wide selection of breads and baked goods and always busy and bustling. I remember seeing Holocaust survivors in the Lincoln Del—especially at the Del on Minnetonka Boulevard. I knew they were survivors because they had the numbered tattoos on their inside forearms. These were people who were in camps during World War II, who had family members that perished, who were persecuted for being Jewish. They had experienced the worst of humanity. And here they were, sitting at the counter next to me eating Hoppel Poppel and reading the paper. That put it all in perspective for me. It wasn't just the soup or the cookies, the breads or the cakes that made the Lincoln Del so very special. It was the people. It was a place that everyone could go to and connect and share in the joy of eating this terrific food."

By historical necessity, the Minnesota Jewish community is very close-knit, its members ranging from the devout Orthodox to the more modern Reform, and these assorted members often unite to fight against the anti-Semitism that still exists today. Because the Del was always "kosher-style," it did carry several kosher items that were produced elsewhere, such as Hebrew National knockwurst. Customers flocked to enjoy once again the flavors and textures they remembered from their Eastern European roots. The Lincoln Bakery gained its popularity and earned respect by

Lincoln
Bakery &
Delicatessen
& Restaurant

Open Sundays
and Holidays

4100 WEST LAKE S
WA 7-9738

Daily for BREAKFAST, LUNCH, DINNER or EVENING
SNACK . . . Delicious Food To Take Home Too!
Northwest finest assortment of Bread, Rolls, Bagel,
Cakes and Pastry. Baked on our own premises.

TOP: *1960 newspaper ad, the first of many.*
BOTTOM: *Lincoln Del at 4100 West Lake*
Street, 1966. Photo by Norton&Peel,
MNHS Collections

"Our Proud Move to the Suburbs":
Lincoln Del East grand opening
announcement, 1957

Grand OPENING

SUBURBIA'S NEWEST and FINEST
BAKERY • DELICATESSEN • RESTAURANT

Wait until you taste our BAKED GOODS

THIS NEW CONVENIENCE FOR SUBURBAN HENNE-
PIN COUNTY IS THE FINEST OF IT'S KIND . . .
ANYWHERE. THE SERVICES AND FOOD OFFERED
WILL BE OF THE HIGHEST CALIBRE. STOP IN TO-
NITE.

GOOD THINGS from our *Delicatessen*

EXCELLENCE IN QUALITY HAS LONG BEEN
STANDARD AT LINCOLN BAKERIES. PERHAPS
YOU HAVE WITNESSED IT YOURSELF AT
EITHER ONE OF OUR OTHER STORES OR AT
SOME OF THE TWIN CITIES FINER RESTAU-
RANTS. SAMPLE OUR BREADS, ROLLS, CAKES
OR SPECIALTIES AND YOU WILL NEVER SET-
TLE FOR LESS.

TAKE THE FAMILY OUT FOR LUNCH OR DINNER. YOU
WILL FIND OUR MENU AS VARIED AND APPETIZING
AS CAN BE FOUND. WE WILL BE OPEN DAILY FROM
7:30 A.M. 'TIL 1:00 A.M. BREAKFAST WILL BE SERVED
DAILY.

IN OUR DELICATESSEN YOU
CAN CHOOSE FROM A HUGE SE-
LECTION OF CANAPES, HORS
D'OEUVRES, COLD CUTS, CAN-
NED DELICACIES, POTATO SAL-
AD, CHEESES OF ALL KINDS.

HOME DELIVERY
CALL YOUR ORDER IN

IF YOU'RE PLANNING A PARTY, YOU WILL BE
HAPPY TO KNOW THAT OUR CATERING DE-
PARTMENT IS STAFFED BY THE MOST EX-
PERIENCED PEOPLE AVAILABLE. CALL IN AD-
VANCE TO DISCUSS YOUR NEEDS . . . YOU
ARE CERTAIN TO BE PLEASED.

CHEESE SPECIALS   BAKERY SPECIALS
CANNED GOODS   QUALITY MEATS
SEA FOODS   FROZEN FOODS

THESE ARE SOME OF THE PEOPLE WHO HELPED MAKE THIS POSSIBLE—

ALLIED EQUIPMENT COMPANY
★ ★ ★
PAULLES FIXTURES
★ ★ ★
WEISEMAN & COMPANY
★ ★ ★
STANDARD PLUMBING
AND HEATING

HOLLICK ELECTRIC
★ ★ ★
MEYERS OUTDOOR
ADVERTISING
★ ★ ★
BESNER CONSTRUCTION
COMPANY
★ ★ ★
ASLESEN COMPANY

HANSEN BAKERY SUPPLY
★ ★ ★
DAIRYLAND MILK CORP.
★ ★ ★
B&B SEAT COVERS
★ ★ ★
SWIFT & COMPANY

WILNO KOSHER PRODUCTS
★ ★ ★
MAAS KEEFE COMPANY
★ ★ ★
ACME LINEN COMPANY
★ ★ ★
KARP'S BAKERS SUPPLY

LINCOLN
4100 MINNETONKA BLVD. ST. LOUIS PARK

• BAKERY
• DELICATESSEN
• RESTAURANT

OPEN DAILY
7:30 A.M.
'til 1:00 A.M.
PHONE WA 7-9738

LINCOLN DEL *Timeline*

1935   1946   1950   1954   1957   1958

LINCOLN BAKERY

1405 Olson Memorial Highway and 2003 Plymouth Avenue North, Minneapolis, opens

Frank Berenberg sells Lincoln Bakery/Lincoln Baking Company to his three sons, Morris, Irving, and Abraham (Robert)

Lincoln Baking Company incorporates

Building and land purchased on Lake Street in St. Louis Park

LINCOLN DEL EAST

(The Joint; Lake Street Del), 4100 West Lake Street (Minnetonka Boulevard), opens

Addition and improvements to Lake Street location

RY OUR DELICIOUS
HOT APPLE PIE
with
CINNAMON ICE CREAM
50c.

New DELICIOUS
diet-rite. cola
LESS THAN **2** CALORIES
PER SERVING
SUGAR FREE

SUNDAES

	.45	HOT FUDGE	.50
CHOCOLATE	.55	HOT FUDGE NUT	.60
CHOCOLATE NUT	.45	CRUSHED CHERRY	.55
CHOCOLATE MARSHMALLOW		CRUSHED CHERRY NUT	.65
CHOCOLATE MARSHMALLOW NUT	.50	CRUSHED PINEAPPLE	.55
CHOCOLATE PEANUT		CRUSHED PINEAPPLE NUT	.65

BREAD, CAKES AND PASTRIES

Constantly Fresh, Constantly Good

THE ONLY DELICATESSEN FEATURING ITS OWN BAKERY RIGHT ON THE PREMISES . . . FRESH BREAD AND ROLLS EVERY HOUR, SEVEN DAYS A WEEK!

Decorated Cakes for Parties and Weddings

LINCOLN BAKERY and DELICATESSEN

At Your Service!

Featuring

VIENNA AND WILNO SAUSAGE PRODUCTS
(OF CHICAGO)

Considered by Experts as the "Best in the Nation"

(NOT RESPONSIBLE FOR PERSONAL PROPERTY)

MAKES HOME ENTERTAINING SUCCESSFUL
AND EASY ON THE HOST

THE HIT OF THE TWIN CITIES

LINCOLN BAKERY AND DELICATESSEN'S

Marvelous

LAZY SUSAN TRAYS

Ideal for

HOME, OFFICE OR SOCIAL GATHERINGS

Containing

SELECTED COLD MEATS
CHOPPED CHICKEN LIVERS
CHOICE ASSORTED CHEESES
FRESH, CRISP SEASONABLE SALADS
OLIVES, PICKLES and RELISHES
ASSORTED ROLLS and BREADS
(BAKED FRESH IN OUR OWN OVENS)

JUST GIVE US A DAY'S NOTICE AND WE WILL
DELIVER PROMPTLY AT THE TIME BEST
SUITED FOR YOUR PURPOSE

LINCOLN

Minneapolis' Most Popular Bakery and Delicatessen

4100 WEST LAKE ST. at HUNTINGTON AVE.

Phone WAlnut 7-9738   Open Daily Including Sunday

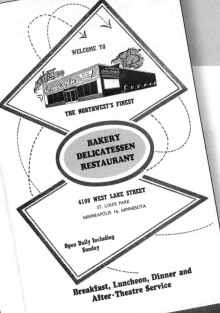

WELCOME TO

THE NORTHWEST'S FINEST

**BAKERY
DELICATESSEN
RESTAURANT**

4100 WEST LAKE STREET
ST. LOUIS PARK
MINNEAPOLIS 16, MINNESOTA

Open Daily Including
Sunday

Breakfast, Luncheon, Dinner and
After-Theatre Service

LINCOLN DINNERS

APPETIZERS

COLD BEET BORSCHT, Sour Cream 50	PICKLED or SCHMALTZ HERRING 65
CHOPPED LIVER 65	Rolls and Butter Included
CHOPPED HERRING 65	GARLIC TOAST (French Bread) .. 30
CHOPPED EGGS with Onions 65	TOMATO JUICE 20
GEFILTE FISH, Horseradish 70	SHRIMP COCKTAIL, Saltines ...1.00
SMOKED FISH 65	
SMOKED SALMON (Lox) 80	HOT BEET & CABBAGE BORSCHT 45

1959 1965 1975 1992 1994 2000

Lincoln Baking Company begins profit sharing plan and trust for all employees

LINCOLN DEL WEST 5201 Wayzata Boulevard at Highway 100 and 12 (now 394), St. Louis Park, opens. This location includes a bar and cocktail lounge.

LINCOLN DEL SOUTH 4401 West Eightieth Street, Highway 494 and France Avenue, Bloomington, opens. This location includes a bar and cocktail lounge.

Lincoln Del Mall of America pop-up holiday store opens in October, selling cookies and gingerbread freshly baked on premises

Lincoln Del West closes as expanded highway system blocks easy access

Lincoln Del closes its remaining locations in Bloomington and St. Louis Park

---

HOT PLATTER SPECIALS

TWO WIENERS and COLE SLAW, Choice of Potato Salad, Sauerkraut or Baked Beans 1.20

FRENCH FRIED SHRIMP, French Fries, Cole Slaw 1.75

SEAFOOD PLATTER SPECIAL, Shrimp, Scallops, Fish Sticks, Cole Slaw, French Fries 1.75

DEEP SEA SCALLOPS, Tartar Sauce, French Fries, Cole Slaw 1.75
Butter and Rolls Included

COLD PLATTER SPECIALS

LINCOLN SALAD 1.50
Shrimp Salad Served on a Nest of Fresh Vegetables, Tomato Wedges, Hard Boiled Egg, Chopped Olives.

WASHINGTON SALAD 1.50
Chicken Salad Served on a Nest of Fresh Vegetables, Tomato Wedges, Hard Boiled Egg, Chopped Olives.

CHEF'S COMBINATION SALAD 1.75
with Turkey, Corned Beef, Swiss Cheese, American Cheese, Tomatoes, Hard Boiled Egg, Olives and Pickles Choice of Dressing.

CHOPPED LIVER, HARD BOILED EGG and TOMATO 1.25

GEFILTE FISH (2 Pieces), TOMATO and LETTUCE, HORSERADISH 1.50

SMOKED FISH, POTATO SALAD, TOMATO and LETTUCE 1.25
Butter and Rolls Included

SIDE ORDERS

INDIVIDUAL HASHED BROWN POTATOES .50
POTATO SALAD .... .35
COLE SLAW .... .25
FRENCH FRIES .... .25
COMBINATION SALAD .... .50

DAIRY SPECIALS

DRY COTTAGE CHEESE and SOUR CREAM .... .65
COTTAGE CHEESE and FRUIT .... .60
Rolls and Butter Included
2 CHEESE BLINTZES, Sour Cream or Jam .95
3 CHEESE BLINTZES, Sour Cream or Jam 1.25
Side of Cottage Cheese .... .35
Side of Sour Cream .... .30

DESSERTS

See Our Special Desserts — Panel on Reverse Side

Chopped Liver Bermuda Onion **1.35**

Pickles, Olives Potato Salad, Rolls and Butter **1.75**

Served with Sherbet or Cottage Cheese Raisin Toast **1.50**

VULTURE ½ Lb. Hollywood Brownburger on French Bread, Raw Onion French Fries and Cole Slaw **1.45**

CANARY ¼ Lb. Hamburger Sandwich Lettuce and Tomato French Fries **.95**

SPAGHETTI with Large Meat Ball Cole Slaw **1.25**
SPAGHETTI & MEAT SAUCE **.85** Includes Garlic Toast

SANDWICHES

CORNED BEEF Hot or Cold
CORNED BEEF and Cole Slaw
CORNED BEEF and Swiss Cheese .... .75
PASTRAMI, Hot or Cold .... .85
TONGUE .... .90
CHOPPED LIVER .... .75
ROAST BEEF .... .75
SLICED TURKEY (All White) .... .65
HARD SALAMI .... .85
SOFT SALAMI 1.15
BOLOGNA .... .70
EGG SALAD .... .60
TUNA SALAD .... .60
SALMON SALAD .... .55
HAM SALAD .... .55
CHICKEN SALAD .... .65
BACON, TOMATO and LETTUCE .... .60
TOMATO and LETTUCE .... .60
AMERICAN CHEESE .... .65
SWISS CHEESE .... .35
PHILADELPHIA CREAM CHEESE .... .40
LOX .... .50
LOX and CREAM CHEESE .... .50
PEANUT BUTTER .... .80
PEANUT BUTTER and BACON 1.20
IMPORTED SARDINE .... .35

HAMBURGER, ¼ Lb. .... .60
CHEESEBURGER .... .75
HOT DOG .... .60
SALAMI or BOLOGNA and EGG .... .70
FRIED EGG .... .40
GRILLED CHEESE .... .85
GRILLED CHEESE and TOMATO .... .45
GRILLED CHEESE and BACON .... .50
GRILLED CHEESE, BACON and TOMATO .... .80
.... .90
5c Extra for Bagel or Kaiser Roll

BEVERAGES

COFFEE .... .10   TEA .... .10
MILK .... .10   ICED TEA .... .10
BUTTERMILK .... ICED COFFEE .... .15

LINCOLN "GOLF CLUB"

SANDWICH SPECIALS

COLUMBIA 1.00
Salami, Swiss Cheese, Tomato and Lettuce

HIAWATHA 1.50
Turkey and Tongue, Tomato and Lettuce

MEADOWBROOK 1.00
Chicken Salad, Bacon, Tomato and Lettuce

OAK RIDGE 1.00
Chopped Liver, Bermuda Onion, Tomato and Lettuce

GOLDEN VALLEY 1.10
Roast Beef, Onion, Tomato and Lettuce

BROOKVIEW 1.15
Corned Beef, Cole Slaw, Tomato, Lettuce with Russian Dressing

LINCOLN 1.20
Corned Beef, Chopped Liver, Tomato and Lettuce

CLUB HOUSE 1.50

Everybody loved breakfast at the Del. This ad announced the opening of the second location in St. Louis Park bordering Golden Valley.

Morrie with his mother, Fanny (Frima Leah, the author's namesake), who only spoke Yiddish, son Danny (age ten), and daughter Penne (age fourteen)

providing high-quality baked goods—and later deli and restaurant items—to the community at large, both Jewish and non-Jewish.

In 1961, Minneapolis elected its first Jewish mayor, Arthur E. Naftalin, who served from 1961 to 1969. And in 1968, Beth El, a congregation comprising some nine hundred families, moved from North Minneapolis to St. Louis Park to join a youth center that had been built at 5224 West Twenty-sixth Street in 1960. Beth El, and the surrounding Jewish community, was within walking distance of Lincoln Del East and Lincoln Del West. Northside Bakery had been started by the Malinsky and Berenberg families in North Minneapolis, and Abe's Delicatessen was there as well, in the same community. Cecil's Delicatessen also appeared in St. Paul.

The Jewish culture of close-knit generations of families and unique gastronomic offerings was not lost on Minnesota's large population of Scandinavians and Eastern Europeans. Many have heartfelt memories of their own Del experiences. Author Karin Winegar was a staff reporter at the *Minneapolis Star* and later the *Minneapolis Star Tribune*. She reviewed restaurants for the *Star* and published, with Joan Siegel, a Twin Cities restaurant guide. She shares the following:

> *When we grew up in the 1960s and 1970s,* our Jewish neighborhood in St. Louis Park encompassed the area between Twenty-sixth Street and Minnetonka Boulevard, then Raleigh Avenue all the way to France Avenue. On Friday nights, especially, you could smell the most wonderful smells coming out of those homes—schmaltz, latkas and brisket. It smelled like home. That's the way the Del smelled—like home. It was like eating memories.
>
> LIZ HERSTEIN SALSBERG

Matzo was our gateway drug. Deep in the Eisenhower era, we lived in a small Minnesota farm town on the Iowa border. It was populated with Germans and Scandinavians, and, to our surprise (we thought they were only in the Bible and Charlton Heston films) there were also Jews: our friends the Gordons, Gendlers, Selzers, and Coopers.

Burt and Charlotte Cooper (pronounced Coopah in her Brooklyn accent) lived across the street, and Charlotte gave my sisters and me our first taste of the faintly sweet, unleavened bread that set us straight on the path to the Lincoln Del and beyond.

She was our mother's shopping pal, and many Saturdays my sister Gayle and I, sometimes with the Cooper girls Beth and Laurie, shot off north to Dayton's in Minneapolis.

One dressed to shop in those days, and Charlotte set the tone in tinkling bracelets, silk scarves, a suit and stockings, big gold earrings, fine leather gloves running well above the wrist and vanishing in the sleeves of her lush wool double-breasted coat with a fur collar. Both mothers sported hairdos rigidly resplendent with Aqua Net, Mom radiating L'Heure Bleue or Shalimar, Charlotte redolent of Estée Lauder or Lanvin.

With Charlotte leading the charge, we romped through Dayton's from shoes (Pappagallos and Capezios) to lingerie ("bend over and *scoop*, honey") to the sacrosanct Oval Room (where Gayle and I played hide-and-seek under the racks of designer clothes), preening and tugging things on and off until we were hungry and whining.

Charlotte chuckled encouragement, pinched our cheeks, and kept us fueled with praise: "You girls are *so gorgeous!*"

Then it was across the street to the Nankin for lunch, where the stout gentleman host ruled the entrance beside a turtle pond stocked with real turtles.

(Chinese for lunch, Jewish for dinner and takeout—no wonder my ex-husband is Jewish. Or as he put it, "I'm only half Jewish, so I'm not a member of the chosen people, but I am a first alternate.")

The day always ended with a triumphant feast at the Del: amid the clatter of dishes and spirals of cigar smoke, we downed corned beef slathered with mustard on dark rye, immense Reubens, steaming chicken soup with matzo balls, cheese blintzes with pots of strawberry jam, sour cream–topped borscht—exotic to kids from the white-on-white Campbell's soup culture.

The Del bustled with talk and interrupting. In our town, there was never such volume, such laughter, such portions, such warmth. (There were rarely olive-skinned brunettes, either. When we first met Charlotte, our only point of comparison was Aunt Jemima on the pancake mix box.) Del meals concluded with monstrous pies and cakes that towered in the deli case: three-tier chocolate cake, chocolate cream pie, skyscrapers of pastry dripping cornices of whipped cream or spires of meringue.

We always took something home for Dad. Into the back of the station wagon went bags of kaiser rolls fragrant with fried onion, glossy poppy seed bagels, loaves of pumpernickel and rye, and a packet of corned beef.

My sister and I were furtive; we were determined. We were, in retrospect, really obvious. By the time the station wagon reached the Minnesota River crossing, we had slid the corned beef out of the bag. By Owatonna the lovely red and white filaments had been peeled away, and half were down the hatch. Fortunately we still had a stash of Fanny Farmer almond bark that was somewhat less plundered.

The Del's magnetism was amplified by the voices of Shelley Berman and Mort Sahl rasping with irony through the gold and tan speakers of our home hi-fi. It was solidified in 1960 with the movie *Exodus* when we all got crushes on Sal Mineo (neither Jewish nor straight, we later learned) and Paul Newman (who was both). Then James Michener's *The Source* (1965)—my first big book—joined the undying influence of Jewish food, Jewish heroism, Jewish humor, and our Jewish friends.

From the beginning, the Lincoln Del was a popular destination for folks throughout the Midwest. Chicago native Jack Apple—rumored to be part of the Midwest Jewish mob—visited the Del regularly and became part of the family. He was godfather to Morrie and Tess's first granddaughter, Wendi. Morrie often invited him over to the Berenberg home on Monterey Avenue in St. Louis Park, not far from the Del.

One time Jack Apple came to the house and told Morrie's daughter Mickey, "There's a present for you in my car." Instead of looking in the back seat where the package was, she went into the glove compartment and found a gun and brought it back into the house. Morrie went ballistic; in those days, Jewish people didn't have guns. (By and large they still don't.) It turned out that Jack was a notorious hit man who'd retired from Chicago. Rick Noodleman remembers that when he left for college, Apple shook his hand: "He had a grip like a vise, and he said, 'Ricky, if you ever need anything, call me.' Fortunately I never had to call him. That's a true story."

Former employee—and still friend of the family—Rollie Troup says that for all his toughness, she never saw Jack Apple hurt anybody. "He had the sweetest wife. They had a collection of fine china cups and saucers, nothing you would think a gangster would appreciate."

Morrie often took his young granddaughter to visit her godfather Jack when he came to town and stayed at the famous Ambassador Hotel. Jack would take out his teeth to tease her, making frightening faces—but he was

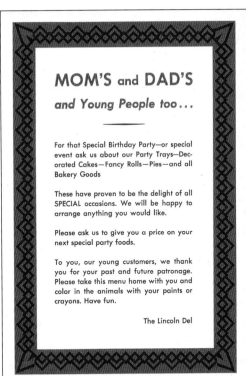

MOM'S and DAD'S

and Young People too...

For that Special Birthday Party—or special event ask us about our Party Trays—Decorated Cakes—Fancy Rolls—Pies—and all Bakery Goods

These have proven to be the delight of all SPECIAL occasions. We will be happy to arrange anything you would like.

Please ask us to give you a price on your next special party foods.

To you, our young customers, we thank you for your past and future patronage. Please take this menu home with you and color in the animals with your paints or crayons. Have fun.

The Lincoln Del

children's
COLORING MENU

THE *Lincoln* DEL

LION
SPAGHETTI
WITH MEAT SAUCE
FRENCH ROLL
$1 55

GIRAFFE
CORNED BEEF
SANDWICH
ON SESAME BUN
WITH POTATO CHIPS
$1 50

BEAR
GRILLED CHEESE SANDWICH
WITH POTATO CHIPS
$1 35

ZEBRA
BROILED HOT DOG
ON A BUN
WITH FRENCH FRIES
$1 75

ELEPHANT
HAMBURGER ON SESAME BUN
WITH FRENCH FRIES
$1 65

SEAL
SUPER SUNDAE . . 50c
CHOCOLATE MILK . 35c
POP (Glass) 35c

UNDER 12 YEARS OLD   EVERYONE GETS A SUCKER

The kid's menu at the Del was iconic—remembered long after young customers had graduated to the adult menu.

always kind to her. And while Jack was living in Minneapolis, none of the Del locations was ever robbed. If Jack was sitting in the Del with Morrie and saw a "disreputable" guy walk in, Jack would get up and escort him off the premises.

Danny Berenberg remembers Jack Apple fondly. Jack took him out when Danny was just a young guy, and because Apple was a convicted felon he couldn't be caught carrying a gun, so he made Danny hold onto it. Danny remembers, "Yes, there I was at sixteen, sitting in a bar with a gun in my lap, sweating out whatever fight was going to happen."

The Lincoln Del was known beyond the Midwest, too—throughout the country and in many corners of the world. For example, after a patron of Katz's Deli in New York City ordered some bagels, she remarked, "These aren't as good as the Lincoln Del's," and the guy behind the counter said, "Oh, the Lincoln Del? I agree with you." Similar conversations still occur in delis on a regular basis.

After so many Jewish families had migrated to the western suburbs of Minneapolis, it became common to take the "road trip" into the city, with the highlight of the day being a stop at Lincoln Del East. Anna Simon grew up in Wayzata and now works as the community relations manager for St. Louis Park's Herzl Camp, attended by many Jewish kids from around the world. Anna shares these memories:

The Del was like home to me . . . like being in my Baubie's kitchen or what I imagine it felt like when you walked into a Catskill resort during summer vacation. You knew everybody. And if you didn't know anyone, someone at your table knew the brother-in-law's mother's cousin of the person sitting next to you. It made me feel so connected to my roots and my history and my community. The Del was part of my Jewish identity and culture.

Every time I walked into the Lake Street Del, my eyes would instantly turn to the display of cakes on the wall. I dreamed of slicing into one of those beautiful princess cakes on my birthday. I imagined the cake would taste like a rainbow or a fairy tale. I stared at those cakes until we had to get in line for the restaurant. As my stomach growled and the line moved forward, my younger brother Jesse and I spied on who else might be there at the Del. Would we see a friend from camp? Would I get a glimpse of my crush? (And would our grandparents know each other? oy! How embarrassing!) Or would we run into a camp counselor or Hebrew School teacher? I savored the aromas and sounds around me.

After we were seated and discussed exactly how we knew (or were related to) every single person in the restaurant, we could finally order. I can close my eyes and see the kids' menu so clearly, I am transported back there in an instant. The Lion—spaghetti and meatballs—was my favorite. Looking back, it was more than just the Lincoln Del food that made an impact on me: it was the atmosphere, it was the experience.

Rabbi Marcia Zimmerman (who officiated at Wendi's wedding in 1986) remembers that when her daughters were little they used to cry during

Passover week because they weren't allowed to have noodles in their matzo ball soup. But they loved the Barbie doll and carousel birthday cakes.

Rollie Troup lived in Cleveland, Ohio, in her twenties, and the first time she visited a deli there called Corky and Lenny's, she told the owners they'd copied the Lincoln Del menu: "They asked me how I knew that, and I said I grew up there; it's the best del ever. I'm the only one who ever said [that] to them. . . . They were so busted." ❤

The Del's fully loaded bakery case. Star Tribune, 1978

*On a rare joint vacation, the Berenberg brothers (Boonie, Morrie, Izzy)
in Palm Springs, early 1970s*

Front of the House

A person can forget everything but eating.
Alts ken der mentsh fargesn not nit esn.
YIDDISH PROVERB

CUSTOMERS OFTEN GATHERED in large numbers at the Del; they never minded standing in line to wait for a table—in fact, that was part of the fun. It was commonplace to see somebody you knew there. The Del was something along the lines of a secular alternative to the church or synagogue. Lincoln Del East, called the "Old Joint" by the Berenbergs, was the flagship location. The St. Louis Park outpost was relocated in 1957 from the original location in North Minneapolis. It began as an on-site bakery facility, retail bakery, and deli. As customers began buying bagels and salami to make their own sandwiches, a coffee shop was added with counter service.

The Berenbergs continued to think of themselves as a bakery company with a restaurant attached. The Lake Street Del's location was in close proximity to the Jewish neighborhoods in St. Louis Park, a popular "first ring" suburb of Minneapolis located minutes from downtown but still with a neighborhood feel. Synagogues and Jewish community centers located in North Minneapolis expanded to other areas of the city and to the nearby suburbs. For St. Louis Park residents, a pedestrian-friendly community linked home, synagogue, grocery stores, and delis. Youngsters could walk to the Del to pick up a challah bread and a cookie after school—often asking the counter staff to "charge it" to their parents' accounts.

The Del was a popular community gathering spot, and regular customers knew what good food meant. There was no way a visit to the Del would go unnoticed. Agnes Berenberg sat you at your table and after saying "hello" would tell you how great your mom looked when she came in for coffee the day before or how well they both had done in mah-jongg the previous night at Tess and Morrie's house, where an animated group of chain-smoking gals gossiped and enjoyed coffee and kmish bread.

Former US ambassador to Morocco Sam Kaplan and his wife, Sylvia,

A typical busy lunch at Lincoln Del East: recognize anyone?

have many fond memories of the Lincoln Del. "Sam always said that the original Del, the one on Lake Street, was the most important because that was where the 'bet din' [rabbinical court of Judaism; Hebrew: בית דין, "house of judgment"] of the Jewish community convened and made important decisions about who was good and who was bad, and what needed to be done to rectify any problem. I miss so many favorite foods; the brisket sandwich on challah bread, the pecan pie, best in the world, are just a couple of examples," says Sylvia.

As crowds of customers waited patiently to be seated, those at the front of the line insisted to the hostess that they must have their regular spot. Those further back in line kibitzed and bragged about their children, or looked at the freezer cases to decide what to take home after their meal. The smell of kaiser rolls, fresh out of the oven, and the delicious aroma of chicken soup filled the air. At the back of the dining room hung a big stuffed swordfish, caught in Acapulco by Tess Berenberg on a rare trip away from the Del. Waitresses weaved through the tables with hot corned beef sandwiches and matzo ball soup, making people studying the menus feel even hungrier than they'd been when they arrived. At the tables closest to the entrance, newcomers grabbed a french fry off a friend's plate or shoved people over to make room. Only rarely did customers sit down immediately—with so many friends and family encountered along the way, there were always folks to talk to and heaping platters to inspect.

Weekly AA groups met regularly in the back, in what used to be the smoking section, under the stuffed swordfish. Izzy Berenberg's own swordfish hung on the back wall of the bar at Lincoln Del West.

Morrie at Lincoln Del East

Tess Berenberg in Acapulco with her prized swordfish catch, later mounted on the wall of the Lincoln Del East.

Culinary maven Sue Zelickson, a local radio, magazine, and online food columnist, says, "The Del was just *the* place to go for breakfast. It was the place to go for lunch or for dinner. There's never been anything like it. Nobody had better bread. We've gone all over the country looking for caraway rye. Nobody does it like the Del did. We've looked in a million places, and you can't find it. You buy it from other bakeries and all the caraway is on the outside; you open it up and there's no caraway inside. The Del would never sell bread made that way."

"So if you went into the East Del on Lake Street, you saw everybody you knew. All the guys used to go there for breakfast every morning and there would be a table of men just sitting around," says Sue. After a stint with the "morning guys," avid listeners would be up on the latest in Jewish community news, pointers on the best investment, the local business report, and advice about the most popular travel destination.

Regulars used the Del as a gathering spot so popular that as one guy got up to leave another immediately took his place at the table, maintaining the ongoing discussion group. High school or college students who showed up for breakfast at the Del with the person they had gone out with the night before were, according to community gossip, officially engaged. It was the farewell huzzah before flying out on some adventure and the first stop on your way home from the airport. Former customer Scott Coleman remembers that whenever his mother came to visit from Rye, New York, she'd insist that they eat at the Del before going anywhere else. "Her father had a Jewish deli in Mount Vernon, New York, so she knew a good deli when she saw one," he says, "and the Lincoln Del was a good one, according to my mom!"

As a Jewish child growing up in a small Iowa town, I frequently traveled with my family to visit relatives for the holidays. We never left for home until stopping at the Del for caraway rye, egg bread, bagels, and corned beef. Some of that never made it back to Iowa. A memory I hold dear to my heart was my father's coffee klatch at the Del weekday mornings. These friends kept my dad [Paul Gruesner] positive and active when facing the dramas of cancer. He looked forward to schmoozing with his friends. The coffee cup was always full and hot. We miss the Del.

ANNE SCHAEFFER

Members of the "Northside reunion" met annually at the Del to talk about the old days and the new, and to learn about the latest family news.

The Del developed special holiday menus and bakery treats for all customers.

WALK FOR *Israel*

THE ANNUAL FUNDRAISER "Walk for Israel" celebrated the creation of the State of Israel, with hundreds walking as many miles as Israel's age. This popular activity was encouraged by the Jewish community centers, synagogues, and groups such as B'nai B'rith Youth Group (BBYO) and United Synagogue Youth (USY). The course went right by Lincoln Del East, and many participants would hang out on the sidewalk there, hoping Morrie's granddaughter Wendi would catch up with them at that very spot and invite them in for a snack to boost their energy to finish the walk. *L*

...at
...resist this perfect combination of
...awberries, ripe blueberries,
...e, grapes, cherries and melon, all
...served in a carved watermelon.
...ctions are seasonal.

...Tray
...ous variety! Sample the best Swiss
...ster, mellow Colby and Sharp
...cheese cubes, plus our unique,
...cheese balls. A center treat of
...Edam finishes this delightful
...ion.

...ay
...eating gourmets will love our array
...d fish, lox, cream cheese, pickled
...ard boiled eggs, olives and
...'s topped off with a center flourish
...rmers Cheese, sour cream and
...heese.

countless times as a kid growing up in the Twin Cities. Often these trips were with my grandfather, who early on taught me the fine art of enjoying great food. In his last years, he suffered from Alzheimer's, but we still managed to get to the Del a few times. It was one of the last places he could recall from a life well lived, and I think going there brought him a sense of peace and security. I will always be grateful for those memories.

MIKE BELL

For the kids of the sixties and seventies, the Del was *the* hangout where everybody gathered—the equivalent of today's coffee shops. Many old friends from high school and college reunited at the Del after they had graduated and gone their separate ways, bringing their spouses and children to enjoy the Lincoln Del experience. For Jewish and non-Jewish customers alike, it was the Minneapolis version of *Cheers*, except that at the Del everybody really *did* know your name. The Del was open every day of the year except one, Christmas.

In fact, Elaine Fries and Bill Johnson were astonished to find the St. Louis Park Del open the morning after the famous Hal-

Celebrating the newly opened Lincoln Del West, Morrie Berenberg holds the most purchased dessert—strawberry shortcake (on right). Minneapolis Star, September 1965

loween storm of 1991. They'd waded the two blocks from their apartment through hip-deep snowdrifts (it was still snowing, and none of the streets had been plowed). Lights were on; the place was packed. Elaine and Bill couldn't believe that cooks and servers were so devoted they'd made it into work and opened up for their customers. Everybody exchanged stories about hiking through the drifts to get to the Del. Staff were cheerful and friendly. They were *there*.

Morrie called himself a "foodaholic." According to an article in a September 1965 edition of the *Minneapolis Star*, "It was nothing for him to polish off an entire cake and two quarts of ice cream, one package each of marshmallow and chocolate cookies, plus two pounds of crackers smeared with peanut butter." This voracious appetite sent Morrie on two month-long trips a year to La Costa Golf and Spa resort in Carlsbad, California, and to the Pritikin Institute (also at that time in California), which he affectionately called the "fat farms," to lose weight. He returned with various healthy recipes, and—with permission from Weight Watchers and Pritikin—incorporated them in the Del menus.

A waitress's legacy: 13 years of chopped liver

Editor's note: The only time most of us think about waiters and waitresses is when something is wrong: The coffee cup is empty, the meat is undercooked, the side order of fried onions missing.

Waiters and waitresses spend their lives smiling even though their feet hurt, being pleasant to cranky customers and hustling for tips from people who may leave anything from $50 to 50 cents as a tip for a $12 meal. Why do they do it? Staff Writer Irv Letofsky interviewed five of them to find out.

Ramona Eicher
Country Kitchen

Mona [for Ramona] Eicher is just about the perfect image for a family restaurant. At 19, a senior at Mounds View High School, she was president of her sophomore and junior classes, a jumping, leaping three-sport cheerleader and a one-time Santa's Helper at the Rosedale Shopping Center.

(She usually is even tempered. She loved the Santa job but, sometimes, the crying children, well, "You just wanna say, shut up and get out of here.")

She is saving up funds for college, perhaps Moorhead State University, perhaps a nursing career.

Ms. Eicher is among the troupe of waitresses at the new Country Kitchen in Roseville, Hwy. 36

and Rice St. She works part-time, some as a waitress at $1.50 an hour plus about once a dollar an hour in tips and some as hostess at $3.10 an hour without tips.

During the summer she worked at a nearby Arby's but counter work was "repetitious." "You would just stand there — 'Can I help you? Can I help you?' The operation was so systematic that after a while I just about drove us crazy.

So she applied at the Country Kitchen and went through the Rosedale training center, where she studied slides on how to wear the orange-and-white-checked aprons, when to bring out the hot and cold cereals, when to fill the cream and pepper shakers, the protocol of punching in, etc.

"Opening day we all got hyper," she remembered. "On my first table I didn't know if the hostess was supposed to bring the menu or me, whether you bring the water or the coffee

Ramona continued on page 10C

Becky Erbes
The Apartment

Becky Erbes, 23, has a well-organized figure that brings honor to her costume — a black, low-cut, tights-like, Bunny-type uniform with sequins and the toe-flattering but otherwise foot-pinching three-inch spiked-heel shoes.

For the noon luncheon at The Apartment, the mostly basement retreat at the Whole House complex in Golden Valley, she circulates in a basic bikini. The management prefers her in the new Rudi Gernreich thong swimsuit and black stockings, but it is "kind of brief" (she says in understatement) and exposes more backside than is comfortable.

Owner Irv Schechtman rejects the term "cocktail waitresses" for the help, preferring Bambi Girls. He looks applicants over for their figures, then instructs the successful ones on the rules of the room.

For example, you don't sit down with customers. You don't smoke or drink. You don't bend over the table. "On a low table," says Becky, "you crouch." Ms. Erbes said "Like a deep knee bend." After the first night there I was pretty stiff."

"Maintain decorum by avoiding slang. 'Certainly' is preferred to 'O.K.,' 'gentlemen' to 'guys.'

And you never date the customers: "Mr. Schechtman wants a certain type of atmosphere and I think wait's appropriate. You could attract the wrong types."

The no-dating policy is a protection: "You get approached twice a night by the regulars." I just tell them that I have a boy friend, which I do. It makes things a lot easier."

(Even regular boy friends aren't allowed in The Apartment. Ms. Erbe's regular, an outdoorsy type, doesn't think much anyway.)

What if the customer is especially attractive?

"I wish you wouldn't ask me that. Besides, they're usually with dates anyway."

Becky continued on page 10C

Michael Brindisi
Promenade Room

For actor-director Michael Brindisi, 27, his recent debut day as the first waiter among the array of waitresses at the Promenade Room of the Sheraton-Ritz Hotel was socko boffo — $22 in tips on top of his $1.72-an-hour salary: "I told almost everybody I waited on that this was my first table."

But the act didn't do as well after that. The average ran to $4.50 a day in tips.

It was his first serious job once he was graduated from Lea Lea College five years ago. But now he and his wife Leslie, who was his first waitress to infiltrate the once all-male Cheshire Cheese restaurant a flight up in the

Michael continued on page 10C

Phyllis Laiderman
Lincoln Del

The chopped liver and chocolate pies at the Lincoln Del are to calories what Rod Carew is to base hits, irresistible.

But Phyllis Laiderman has spent 13 years in and around the chopped liver and chocolate pies and the Del at 4100 W. Lake St., St. Louis Park, and has maintained a reasonable girth. It is difficult to comprehend.

"Customers tell me I'm so lucky because I'm thin," she said. "Well, first of all, I'm not that thin. But you find that you just eat lighter when you're working. All the waitresses. I don't know why.

Phyllis continued on page 10C

Lorraine Heath
Gay 90s

"I don't know why I like it," said Lorraine Heath on the chosen profession. "I just get tense every night. But I like meeting people. Even if I could tend office work, I wouldn't. It would be too monotonous."

She is among the fixtures of antiquity in the Gay 90s, the relic nineties-bar-restaurant that recently turned discotheque on Hennepin Av. off 9. 4th St. One of the best waitresses I've ever seen ... said manager Dick Golst ... steady, dependable, efficient, intelligent.

She spent about 38 of her 55 years in the service business, the last 15 at the Gay 90s, usually at the front 10 tables and game room. Back many years ago, she started her career a little Franklin Av. coffee shop, the name of which she has long forgotten.

Mrs. Heath has developed her vocation into a serious art form. She is so precise that, for example, she lays drink orders on the bartender in a fixed sequence so that he can pour more neatly right to left, according to kinds of his liquors, bourbons, gins and others. It is a tribute to proficiency.

Lorraine continued on page 10C

Phyllis Laiderman "spent over thirteen years in and around chopped liver and chocolate pies and has maintained a reasonable girth. It is difficult to comprehend. 'Customers tell me I'm so lucky because I'm thin,' she said. 'Well, first of all, I'm not that thin. But you find that you just eat lighter when you're working. All the waitresses. I don't know why. But there's not a dessert here that I don't love today as much as I did when I started.'" Minneapolis Tribune, October 9, 1975

In an effort to stay healthy, Morrie walked around Lake Calhoun twice a day. He continued his exercise routine at the Berenberg winter home in Scottsdale, Arizona. The family dog, Love, accompanied him—and then slept the rest of the day to recover.

Audrey Wilcox worked at the West Del in the early 1980s. "Morrie walked in the back door, through the bar to meet his friends for dinner. . . . One night as he walked by, he said to me, 'Don't ever get fat.' It was around the time he had been walking every day around Lake Calhoun and had lost weight. I never knew him when he was heavier. I think most people were afraid of him when he came in, but he was always nice to me."

Lincoln Del employees were loyal, with strong work ethics. The waitresses were professionals; they made careers in the restaurant business. Serious about their work, Del employees knew what they were doing and took pride in what they served. In that different time, Morrie Berenberg insisted on a strict dress code: "You have to cut your hair, you can't have tattoos, no pierced ears."

Even so, people worked at the Del for years. The Lincoln Del employees came from all walks of life, and from the 1930s North Minneapolis wholesale bakery to the day the St. Louis Park and Bloomington Dels closed their doors in 2000, these loyal employees were treated as equals in the business—as family. Many employees were able to buy houses or put their children through college with funds they earned from the Berenbergs' profit-sharing program. If the Berenbergs learned that an employee faced dire financial times, they often quietly paid medical bills, mortgages, and college tuitions. To them, it's just what a good employer did. The dishwasher Fed—famous for sitting on empty milk crates under the employee punch-in machine as he dug into huge bowls of butter-laden mashed potatoes—commanded the same respect as the truck drivers, bakers, prep cooks, chefs, servers, and Morrie and Tess themselves.

One member of the immediate family, Agnes Berenberg, helmed the cash register at the original Del on West Lake Street. Her son, Frank Richard Noodleman, named for his grandfather and better known as Rick, started working there when he was about twelve, folding pie and cake boxes behind the counter. He continued to work at the Del during summers and on weekends until he left for Harvard. (The Harvard desk chair he brought back for Uncle Morrie sat proudly in the Lake Street basement office.)

"I did everything," he remembers. "I worked behind the counter, I worked as a cashier, as a host, I was a busboy, and drove the truck a bit. So you know, it was the place to be. On any given day, most of the people you knew would walk in there to buy something or to eat or get a loaf of bread from the bakery. It was like old home week or a dance or a school event."

His wife, Arlene, recalls, "Rick and I grew up a block and a half from each other in St. Louis Park, and the Del was only a block and a half away. So when I was turning sixteen, I thought hey, it's five blocks away or whatever it was—Twenty-sixth to Thirtieth—and I'd been going there all my life, I thought, 'I'll try to get a job there.' That was my first job ever in high school, and Rick was working there because of his uncle Morrie, and everybody else in the family worked there, too.

"After my first year of college, Rick was graduating from high school, and Agnes kept saying, 'Ricky got into Harvard,' and I said to somebody, 'You know, it's really great that Rick got into Harvard, but why is Agnes so excited about it?' And this woman said, 'Well, don't you know that's his mother?' Because Rick is such a discreet sort of person, I had no clue that he was related to everybody there, practically. His mother and his cousin Freddie [Izzy's son] were in the bakery, and his uncles Izzy and Boonie were in the bakery in the back making bagels, and Freddie was in the front with the cakes and I had—I had no clue. It just blew me away that I was working with this guy for almost two and a half years and I had no idea because he was never one to brag."

Rick continues, "I'll tell you a couple of stories. There was a time when my uncle Morrie, as he liked to do, was holding court in the restaurant, and he was situated so he was just behind the pie case and he'd be looking toward the front part of the restaurant where the cashier area was. He was ostensibly watching the place, and he would meet with different suppliers and business people and customers that he knew would come in and sit down at his table and chat with him. One day during the winter, these two guys walk in with heavy overcoats, and one of them is carrying a briefcase, and they both have these bushy beards. Like on the cough drops, you know, the Smith Brothers picture on the package.

"So they walk in, and my uncle remarks to whoever is sitting next to him at his table, 'Here come the Smith Brothers.' Well, the Smith Brothers went downstairs, where on your left was a bathroom and on your right was an unmarked door that was the office. Apparently the Smith Brothers knew that that was the office, so they let themselves in and Margaret, who was Tom Friedman's mother, was in there with Ralph, the senior bookkeeper.

"So they're in the office working, and the Smith Brothers go in there, and they rob the place. They tie up Margaret and Ralph, they break into the safe and steal about $10,000, and they come back up the stairs. And as they go by, Morrie says, 'There go the Smith Brothers.' Well, the Smith Brothers walked out of there with all that money. They never got caught, and the police never found the money. And that's the story of the Smith Brothers."

> *In the 1970s this was a must every time my mom,* sister, and I trekked from Hutchinson, Minnesota, to the Cities for shopping, a ballet, etc., with other family and friends. We'd all pack into the station wagon or Buick or Olds, and in we'd come. The favorite entrée was, hands-down, french dip sandwich with the great pickle and fries and a chocolate malt. On the way out, my mom would have to stop in the bakery area and take home a loaf or two of the dark pumpernickel bread and rolls. I can smell the warm pumpernickel roll after coming out of the microwave and spreading some butter on it. I miss that to this day!"
>
> **RHONDA TEICH HICKEY**
> remembering stopping at the
> **West Del on old Highway 12**

Another story starts with Rick's mother, Agnes Berenberg, standing at the cash register as she did every morning. Many of the regulars bet on sports—football, baseball, horse racing—and often they'd use the company phone. There was a pay phone right by the stairs to the bathroom, and there were a couple of business phones at the cash register, but of course everyone liked to use the free phones. Bookmakers placed their bets, and it turns out that the authorities—Rick didn't know if it was the federal authorities or who it was—were watching the place. So at about ten o'clock one morning the police pulled up in front of the Del with three paddy wagons, and they arrested everyone in the place. Rick got pulled from his junior high class to the principal's office to hear, "Your mother's been arrested." She was out by noon because, obviously, they knew she had nothing to do with it. She spent the morning in jail, this wonderful Jewish woman.

Agnes was the hostess and cashier stationed near the front door. Next to the cash register was a large cigar case. It would get dirty, what with the tobacco and the dust of the cigars, and she insisted that the staff keep it clean. Agnes was meticulous. The staff would have weekly cleaning assignments, and she'd make them take the screws out of the glass cases to clean them. When it was slow, they'd pull the glass out of the cigar case and from the one where the French pastries were kept, where frosting had smeared on the glass. For some reason, Agnes particularly liked the way her future daughter-in-law Arlene cleaned it, and she'd call to Arlene, "Honey . . ." Arlene avoided her because she didn't want to clean that case all over again. Agnes had a huge beehive, and she wore blue glasses and strange shoes that were probably orthopedic oxfords. Arlene was afraid of her. Agnes ruled the roost at the Del, keeping the front of the house running smoothly. She was fair but firm, hardly the pussycat she became in private with her family.

Kate O'Brien Bronson recalls:

I began working at the Lincoln Del the day after my fourteenth birthday. My mother was the bookkeeper, and my brother worked in the prep kitchen. I am the only person who held the job title of toast maker as far as I know. I was a "gofer," fountain prep, bakery/deli clerk, prep cook, catering assistant, and finally office assistant. I loved the atmosphere, the customers, and the food. I still have cravings for the Delwich, Edna's potato salad, and the knishes.

One of my more favorite memories happened in the deli. I was in the middle of a ten-hour shift, it was a busy weekend afternoon, and we were falling behind on filling the sample tray. I glanced up at a customer who stopped by the tray, empty but for ice, and he asked, "What are we sampling today?" Not missing a beat, I blurted out, "Hand-chipped ice carved from the French Alps." Feeling rather proud of my quick wit, I looked again at the guest, who was now laughing, and I nearly passed out. It was Soupy Sales [comedian Milton Supman]. The Del served celebrities both local and national.

I learned patience and customer service. Thanks to Danny, Izzy and Boonie, Mickey, Brian, Jimmy, Edna, Georgia and the parking lot ducks, Tess and Morrie, I am now a culinary instructor, chef, caterer, and event planner.

And from Paula Lichter Shapiro:

The Lincoln Del was a Saturday night ritual. It was where to see people and where to be seen with wonderful memories of good friends and family. I have lived in Texas now for forty-eight years. I brought my children to Minnesota when they were young to show them all the fabulous places I enjoyed growing up. We went from the airport DIRECTLY to the Lincoln Del. I remember eating the wonderful soups, especially, if I remember correctly, the barley soup. Many years ago the *Jewish World* printed the recipe for the Hot Cabbage Borscht, another one of my favorites, and I make it to this day. So many memories but, for some reason, the onion pletzel sticks out in my mind—enjoying it on Sunday morning at the kitchen table with my parents. . . . I used to buy one every Saturday night, and we would have it the next morning for breakfast. It was flat like a pizza and covered with onions. If I concentrate, I can still taste it. I live in Texas now, but I will never forget my fond memories of the Lincoln Del.

P.S. A small anecdote you probably would not like to share in the book. An older waitress was clearing the table next to us. She lifted a glass of iced tea, held it up, looked it over, and took a sip. We laugh about that still today.

Dick Bernard shares this touching story:

Kindness to a young teacher. My wife and I came to Minneapolis in 1965. We were from rural western North Dakota. We had never been to the Twin Cities. She was dying of kidney disease, and the last hope was University Hospital for a kidney transplant. She was twenty-two; I was twenty-five. I was a teacher, we had no insurance, I had no money, we had a year-old son. Somehow or other I found out about a job in the deli section of the Lake Street Lincoln Del and was hired sometime in June. When I first came to the restaurant, I doubt that I had ever met someone Jewish, much less known about things like kosher. But I learned the products and customer service.

There are three people who were memorable to me: Blanche Finkelstein and a rotund man whose name I just cannot recall [probably Marv Shedlov, who lived across from the Berenbergs on Monterey Avenue just blocks from the Lake Street Del] were behind the counter and taught me the basics. They were always there. Sam Weiner was the maître d'. They helped me survive that awful summer. I am forever grateful to them.

For a month or so I lived in a single room on University Avenue not far from U Hospital. Our son had gone back to North Dakota to stay with relatives. On July 24, my wife died before receiving a transplant. She was very, very sick. On the same day that Medicare became U.S. law, she was buried in Valley City, North Dakota. Three days before she died I had been hired as a teacher in Anoka-Hennepin [School District]. When school began in the fall, I was broke; my son and I lived with a family in Anoka, and I commuted to a second job at Lincoln Del. I put in quite a number of hours, especially weekends. The family took care of my son.

At one point in time I bought an entire chocolate pie and endeavored to eat it all. I lusted after it! I couldn't finish it. For some reason I remember the very, very well-aged kosher dills stored in the basement. I got to be pretty good at estimating weight of sliced corned beef, etc. That was a useful talent.

Sometime that fall of '65 the new Lincoln Del was opened on Wayzata Blvd, and I was among the folks who worked behind the counter there. My career, though, turned out to be short. In January of 1966, I came down with pneumonia—probably exhaustion was the cause—and I had to quit the job at Lincoln Del. Life went on as life does; things got better; most of the subsequent years I could occasionally go to Lincoln Del as a customer, including the last restaurant off 494. . . . If Lincoln Del were still around, I'd still be going there from time to time. ♥

LATE NIGHT *Noshing*

DANNY BERENBERG worked with his friends Dave Mona and Paul Maccabee, both legends in the world of Twin Cities public relations, to promote the Del in many ways. When the Del wanted to remind its customers that it was the best late-night nosh spot, Dave delivered with a creative letter to Pat Lindquist of *Skyway News*.

Dear Pat:

After 1 a.m. the vampires do not come out at the Lincoln Del restaurants—but the lemon meringue and corned beef reubens sure do!

In the last month alone, Pat, Danny Berenberg's Lincoln Del restaurants have been honored by *Twin Cities* magazine as the area's #1 locations for "Late Night Noshing" and featured in the *Star Tribune* as a mecca for after-midnight dining. Explained Danny to the *Tribune*—"We're doing a public service. You wouldn't expect an emergency room to shut its doors at 11 p.m., would you?"

What's behind this nocturnal noshing at the Del? Danny suggested you might wish to share with your *Skyway News* readers some exclusive inside stories about the moonlit denizens of the Del.

You already know that all three Lincoln Del locations are open until 2 a.m. on Friday and Saturday nights. "That means we do not turn our grills off at 2 a.m.," says Danny. "It's our philosophy that if you dash through our door by 2 a.m., you can order anything on the menu."

According to Danny, the Lincoln Del welcomes a flood of post-midnight police officers (just getting off the evening shift), hospital emergency room nurses, waitresses from other restaurants, taxi cab drivers, and pro athletes from the North Stars, Strikers and other teams.

Perhaps because of its proximity to Rupert's nightclub on Highway 12, the Lincoln Del West in St. Louis Park enjoys a flood of starry-eyed post-1 a.m. "we just met" singles. "You'll see lots of couples who just hit it off on the dance floor at Rupert's and then use the Lincoln Del as their testing ground for new relationships," says Danny slyly. "By today's rules of dating etiquette, I guess it's safe for a woman to accept a man's late-night invitation to share a cheese blintz!"

Celebrities who've dropped by for late-night Del dining have included Sammy Davis, Jr., Senators Rudy Boschwitz and David Durenberger, Dick Van Dyke, Rodney Dangerfield, David Brenner, Pia Zadora, Don Shelby and Pat Miles of WCCO-TV and Steve and Sharon Anderson of KSTP-TV.

After 1 a.m., the sale of breakfast items soars—particularly cheese omelettes and hash browns. Also enormously popular with late-night munchers is lemon meringue pie.

But after 1 a.m., it appears that many Lincoln Del diners have relaxed their inhibitions beyond mere pie. "How else can you explain our business at that time in weird combinations?" says Danny. "For example, we get requests for matzo ball soup with lemon wedges and tomato ketchup. Others ask for our spicy cabbage borscht ordered with chocolate pie. They never ask for that combination during the day!"

And when customers crave late-night deli food, they will let nothing stop them. Berenberg was astounded during this year's savage rainstorms when late-night diners slogged through hip-deep water and mud to reach their appointed Del destination. "We had people coated with storm debris up to their waists . . . finding refuge from the storm with a bagel."

Danny recalls that 10 years ago, the Minneapolis gambling dens would send their runners to the Lincoln Del at 1:30 a.m. for "tons of corned beef sandwiches and pie." The Del still regularly flies pieces of lemon meringue pie to a casino in Las Vegas.

And then there are Danny's real 1 a.m. oddballs. "One insurance man burst into the Lincoln Del South at 1:10 a.m. and asked for one piece of every single dessert in the restaurant," marvels Danny. "But my God, we bake and sell some 100 desserts. He packed $500 worth of sweets into his car and drove off at 1:40 a.m."

Another popular customer confessed to a private fantasy of stuffing himself in the Lincoln Del after closing time. "So we fed him until 4 a.m. an unbelievable amount of food. Five orders of corned beef hash. Half a cherry cheesecake. It was astonishing," chuckles Berenberg.

To satisfy the rising tide of late-night noshers, the Lincoln Del is offering late-night specials— including a free cup of matzo ball soup with every corned beef sandwich, half off every grilled reuben, and all desserts only $1.49. "Most restaurants abandon food so they can make more money on liquor late at night. We operate in reverse," says Danny.

Of course, Danny would be glad to provide more twilight eating anecdotes for your column . . . L

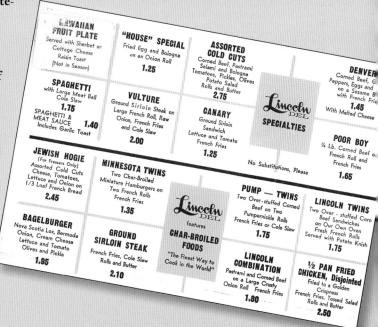

A view from the north of the cocktail lounge and back entrance at Lincoln Del West.

Back of the House

The smell of good bread baking, like the sound
of lightly flowing water, is indescribable
in its evocation of innocence and delight.
M. F. K. FISHER

Any time a person goes into a delicatessen
and orders a pastrami on white bread,
somewhere a Jew dies.
MILTON BERLE

THE BERENBERGS thought of themselves primarily as bakers; the deli and restaurants came later. The brothers were large, strong men. They could carry hundred-pound sacks of flour, one under each arm. Baking was hot, hard, dirty work, especially in the summers and before air conditioning. When the ovens were fired, kitchen temperatures could exceed 120 degrees, which is why the bakers worked at night, when it was cooler. And even after the kitchens were air-conditioned, the Berenbergs baked at night so their product would be fresh for the morning rush.

Gale "Stormy" Strommer was a baker at the Del from 1962 to 1963, working with Boonie Berenberg (Strommer called him "Bob") at the ovens for a year and a half. He says everybody was proud of working at the Lincoln Del. Many of the older employees had grown up during the Depression and were just glad to have a job. Strommer remembers, "The Berenbergs were gods. And if you were loyal, they were very generous." Boonie Berenberg was especially good to him: "I have nothing but great memories of him. I can honestly say I loved the guy. I really did."

He says, "Accountability is so important. So many of these business owners today should really learn that if the consistency and quality isn't even, your customers won't come back. At the Del, it was quality all the way. We knew that, we never doubted it. The only way you're successful is if you can develop a system to guarantee your quality. If you buy a product on Monday it has to be just as good the next time you buy, say, on a Saturday. If a product wasn't right, you didn't serve it, or if a customer didn't like it, you sent it back, no questions asked. Consistency was key; it had to taste the same on Saturday as it did on Wednesday."

The Berenbergs understood the process of fermentation—one of the reasons their product tasted so good and had so much flavor. Here's the secret: to bake Jewish bread with a sour, make it up the day before and put it in the refrigerator. This period of rest allows it to mellow itself out and the flavors to meld. You need twenty-four hours in the refrigerator to retard the dough. That extra step makes a world of difference.

Another key to success was that the Berenbergs baked four times each day. The night crew did the first bake for delivery to accounts off-site. Strommer would arrive at 8:00 AM, by which time the first bake was already done and out the door. Then they would start preparing the next bake so that when the Del opened the bread and the rolls were always hot and fresh for the first customers. Next bake was in time for the noon lunch crowd, which was huge, and then they'd do another one after Boonie saw what had sold at lunch. Boonie kept track intuitively: "'We'll need two more caraway rye, we'll need two more white rye, we'll need six more pumpernickel.' He was amazing. Then you'd have another bake, and we'd probably get that out

4:30, 5:00 for the supper crowd. And later the night crew would come in and start all over again. Seven days a week."

At that time, the Berenbergs made only three kinds of bagels: sesame, poppy, and plain, as many as a hundred dozen a day. They baked them four times a day, so they were always fresh. Sometimes there might be five or six bakes for the bagels. "Bob would say, 'We only got time for six pans right now,' and so we'd just do six pans, fill the store, get the other stuff, and be thawing the others out in six more pans. . . . We had eighteen pan ovens, both the red oven and the other oven with eighteen pans, so you had four

Making bagels. Izzy Berenberg at far left

Izzy making bagels

dozen bagels to a pan. That's how we figured everything out. When you run an oven like that, at that scale where you've got so much to do, you learn to time things and go do this, and that'll come out in eight minutes, then we get our bread in.

"Anybody that worked out front, they'd say, 'Hey somebody just came in and bought two dozen kaiser rolls. Now we only got two dozen left.' Boom, away you went. It was a good system. They tried as much as possible to keep it fresh, keep it full. Nobody does that anymore. Everybody bakes it on Monday and sells it on Friday. Izzy Berenberg made the best kaiser rolls in the business.

"They made everything fresh every day. The Danish, beautiful Danish, oh my god—best Danish I've ever eaten. It was that good. They used huge blocks of butter. The first thing I saw when I walked into the bakery was this fifty-pound block of butter. The Berenbergs didn't bother with smaller quantities; they didn't have time. The streusel was made with honey and butter and flour, a little salt. Everything was rich. When the Danish would come out of the oven we'd brush it with honey glaze—that helps keep it from drying up. So we'd put the glaze on with a brush, and then we'd ice it. Nowadays you just bake it, ice it, and put it in the pack. They don't bother glazing it. Another thing that's changed, and this might be interesting, we baked it dark. I like it that way, with a little crunch. This is one of the problems I've had my whole life since: every once in a while when I went to other jobs, they insist, 'That's too dark.' I'd say, 'No, it's not.'"

Morrie was a great businessman. Strommer remembers that they made fruit tarts one day, "And they were good—nice little fruit tarts. They didn't sell. They were fifteen cents and they did not sell. Morrie came in the next day and he said, 'Well, they're too cheap, charge twenty-five cents.' They sold. True story.

"One time I got burned real bad. I had been there a month, and I was taking a pan out of the oven. We put the bagels on the rack, I hadn't been there long, and I was a little confused. I turned wrong, and I burned my arm. Made a big scar; it's gone now, but it was there for a while. Boonie almost cried. 'You little schmuck, you gotta be careful. Come here now let me look at that.' We ran to the sink and washed it off and dried it. We actually didn't put any Band-Aids on it. He said, 'It'll be better if it air dries.' Heart of gold. I never had a problem with Boonie. We got along good. He was a sweetheart.

"I learned how to run a bakery from the Berenbergs, but I didn't realize it until I was thirty years old. . . . One day I said, 'Wow.' The light bulb turned on, and I said, 'God, I learned this—all this—from the Lincoln Del.' Yeah, I had four kids, and seven grandkids, and two great-grandchildren. They've all done real well, and it's all because I had enough brains not to holler about seventy-five cents an hour and Boonie saw something in a hundred-pound little kid. I don't know what he saw in me, but he took a liking to me. Something clicked in there, in like five minutes. I

Many Lincoln Del employees were real characters. One of the chefs was a bit of a hothead, and the galley kitchen at the Lake Street Del was relatively small for the volume of food they produced. One night in the 1960s, two of the cooks got into an argument, and one of them went to the back parking lot to his car and got a gun, came back into the kitchen, and started trying to hit the other guy. Bullets ricocheted around the kitchen, and Izzy Berenberg had to deal with it. The guy wouldn't give Izzy the gun. Eventually Izzy, being a big guy, calmed him down and got the gun.

just put my head down, but at the same time they taught me. They liked me, and they taught me. I loved it. It was my first real job."

The Berenbergs were far from well behaved at times. When Robert "Boonie" Berenberg was a teenager, he was quite the late-night carouser. The young baker was supposed to show up for his 2 AM shifts at the bakery, but one time he came in late, and he had these huge ovens with hundreds of dozens of bagels rotating, and he was tired, so he stretched out on the bench and fell asleep. When he woke up of course all the bagels were toast, and he knew that his father, Frank, would kill him. Frank was known to be a "tough son of a bitch," Rick Noodleman remembers. So Boonie hopped a freight train to Chicago. He was nineteen. It's unknown exactly how long he stayed there, but when he came home, he morphed into his father, standing in the back of the bakery in a white t-shirt and with a cigar in his mouth. He was gruff but had a heart of gold.

Boonie had a series of pets, Boston terriers, and he called them all Jake. Danny Berenberg named his son Jake, as he was very fond of Morrie's best friend, Jake Garber. The joke was that Danny named his son after Boonie's prized terriers. So when somebody in the family mentioned "Jake," you didn't know whether you were talking about Jake the dog or Jake the boy. Boonie had about six of those dogs, and the last one had front legs that didn't flex, so he looked like he was goose-stepping.

Boonie lived in the house that bordered the back parking lot of Lincoln Del East, an easy commute. He'd walk to work, go home, eat dinner, go to sleep. He did that until his retirement at sixty-five.

Morrie's granddaughter Wendi and her friends made many impromptu visits to the back bakery's huge walk-in refrigerator, where they would dip strawberries in the bucket of strawberry glaze. Wendi's friend Robin Melemed Gale remembers "getting to walk in the back through the KITCHEN with Tooda, aka Wendi, sitting down in the restaurant, and after we were done eating she would sign the back of the check with 'thanks Zadie.' We were so stinkin' cool."

Rabbi to the Baker

ON THURSDAYS, the Berenbergs donated an oven-load of bread to their synagogue, Beth El. The bread was made especially for survivors of the Holocaust. Their digestive systems had been damaged in the camps, and they couldn't eat soft (i.e., gooey or doughy) bread. So this bread was baked for the usual twenty-five minutes at 425 degrees, then for another twenty to thirty minutes at 200 degrees. Gale Strommer remembers this story.

Well, this was the summer of 1963, and I was eighteen years old. I was running late, and I had plans for that evening. So instead of drying out the bread at 200 degrees, I kept the oven on high at 425 degrees, and when it looked kinda dark enough, I took it out of the oven. So it looked crisp on the outside, but it was soft on the inside.

So the next morning, when I walked into work, no one talked to me in the whole place. No one said a word; no one looked at me or acknowledged me in any way. I thought, "Oh, boy. Here we go. I'm ostracized here." I knew what I did was wrong. I had no excuses. I didn't *make* any excuses, but being young and dumb (at eighteen, my IQ was about eighteen), I shrugged it off.

Well, in the course of the morning, Boonie, Izzy, and Morrie each chewed me out real good. That afternoon, in walks a rabbi just like on TV, all in black with a scraggly beard, and this is how it went:

RABBI: You da goy?
ME: Yes, I am.
RABBI: You come to me.
ME: All right.
RABBI: The soggy bread you did?
ME: Yes.
RABBI: I am ashamed to be standing next to you.

He pulls up his sleeve and shows me the number on the inside of his wrist, the tattoo from the concentration camp.

RABBI: You know dis?
ME: Yes.
RABBI: Den dis makes it the worstest.

He then proceeded to tell me what he thought of me, and when he was done I felt so small, I could have walked upright under a closed door. I'm ashamed of myself now, but at eighteen I'd barely heard of the Holocaust—I'd quit school, I never had much education. I just didn't know. I did a good job on the bread the next Thursday, and on Friday the rabbi stopped in and he said, "Not so good as Boonie, but is okay." And about a month later he came by again and said, "Is good, goy, is good." That made me feel better, but I still feel ashamed about the way my actions had disappointed such a good man. *L*

Bakery Production, a trade magazine, featured the Lincoln Bakery operations in their April 1974 edition. The article described baking techniques and celebrated the brilliant Doll Katzovitz Laboe, who delighted in creating her famous designs, which included the popular bikini cake, Snoopy's doghouse cake, and even a yellow smiley face with braces cake inspired by a round pin Morrie's granddaughters brought home from a visit to the orthodontist. Doll eventually opened up her own bakery—It Takes the Cake—with her husband, Jack Laboe. She had the Berenbergs' blessing, along with

incoln Del Bakery

cream cakes and other cream desserts." Morrie still keeps one eye on production, always looking for a way to make something better. Only recently he acquired his new cheese cake formula which, made without "baker's" cheese, has a higher ingredient cost than his old formula, but produces a superior cake. Since the changeover, sales of cheese cake have continued to increase, until today, the bakery uses over 500 lb. of cream cheese a week, just for cheese cake!

BREAD VARIETIES— BIGGEST SELLERS

Each bread and roll variety is made to have its own distinct taste appeal. For them, the bakery uses only freshly-milled, full-flavor rye and pumpernickel flours, high-protein patent, clear and high-gluten flours, fresh eggs, butter, vegetable oil and the bakery's own preferment sour that Morrie claims to be even older than he.

Lincoln Del's distinctive variety breads are the bakery's biggest production items. Not only does bread account for a full 25% of the bakery sales, but the restaurants' high volume in sandwiches creates extra demand.

Morrie takes particular pride in Lincoln Del's breads. "Good bread and average meat still makes a good sandwich" is an axiom he has long believed.

Production of rye and pumpernickel breads is a high-volume business. To make the doughs, two starter sours are used—one for the 3 rye varieties, the other for the pumpernickel. A sizeable piece of fermented dough is held over each day to become the "starter" for the next day's production.

About noontime each day, Bill hand-mixes the two "wet" sour starters, using white rye in one and pumpernickel in the other. Each sour is made with about 2 gal. of water, 10 lb. of flour and half of the leftover dough.

When the dough mixer comes in at

1. As rye dough pieces come out of the molder of the bread system, they are arranged on cornmeal-dusted peel-boards ready for proofing and baking.

2. Part of each day's made-up hearth varieties is rolled into the cooler to be retarded for bake-off the following morning. Until defatted soy flour was added to each dough, retarded rye doughs initially had "fish-eye" blisters on the crust after baking.

3. Proofed loaves are baked on the hearth in one of two side-by-side reel

At Lincoln Del Bakery with our editors

ovens, each piped with low-pressure steam.

4. Distinctive quality and eye appeal are evident in this selection of Lincoln Del's bread varieties.

5. Restaurant quality in rolls and bagels is more than just a term since these items are served in the restaurant as well as offered in the bakery.

their recipes for challah and several pastries. Jack experimented with delicious knishes, and Doll continued to create her own wonderful recipes and incredible cakes that were highly sought after by many private and corporate clients. It Takes the Cake was always the "go-to" bakery for her creative birthday, bar and bat mitzvah, wedding, and special-event cakes.

Pastry chef Daniel Hemiadan brought his European-trained talents to the Del, and his incredible, delectable creations delighted Del customers. He made one-of-a-kind items that were showstoppers at national pastry

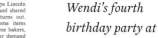

Above left, baker loads bread dough into hopper of divider in one-man bread make-up line, which includes rounder, proofer and molder.

Top right, exterior of original Lincoln Del, remodeled in 1971 includes off-street parking at right and behind bakery.

Above right, displaying some of Lincoln Del's items are, l. to r., Arnie Orloski, managing editor of Bakery magazine, Morrie Berenberg, pres., and Baker Editor Frank Gruber of Bakery magazine.

Many product ideas come from the customers themselves, either housewife recipes or items people have tried in other areas. Both Morrie and Bob keep alert for new ideas when they travel or visit other bakeries.

"Like a big restaurant menu, I believe you can't afford to cut variety too much," Morrie says, "or you begin to back out of the business. When you're in business to satisfy customers, you have to have the products they want."

Because bakery products serve both restaurant and bakery customers, eye appeal is critical, Morrie says. He believes the appearance of an item is one of its strongest merchandising features.

"No matter how good a product tastes," he says, "it's how it looks that really sells them."

Variety and appeal are particularly important because Lincoln Del continually watches individual product performance. "When sales of a particular product start to fall off," says store manager Bruce Hedenland, "we quit producing it for awhile. After a few weeks, we bring it back and promote it heavily."

Lincoln Del's Harvey Wallbanger cake is a good example. When sales started to drop off, it was eliminated for several weeks. When it was again offered with in-store promotion, sales climbed to 150 cakes per weekend, higher than ever before!

The same attention and skill are paid to display location in the store. Coffee cakes sell best when displayed on the eye-level shelves above the display cases, Bruce says. Very few items are packaged before display. However, cookies and a few loaf cakes sell well when packaged and displayed in the store's island merchandiser.

TOP INGREDIENTS MOST IMPORTANT

The most important facet of variety, Morrie believes, is emphasizing retail specialty products, not wholesale-type

items.

Quality is not hard to attain provided the right ingredients are used, says Morrie, which is perhaps Lincoln Del's secret to the big demand shared by everything the bakery turns out. The ingredient cost of some items would be prohibitive for some bakers, but at Lincoln Del, customer demand for an item is established in the restaurant before it is offered at retail. In fact, very few items are made solely for retail bakery sale.

Bill Haegler, a 14-yr. veteran, trained well under Morrie Berenberg while the "boss" was still engaged in production, is in charge of bakery operations at Lincoln Del, assisted by a crew of 12 craft bakers, one lady decorator and 3 apprentices.

Baking operations start about midnight in order to have a full line of fresh-baked items for the restaurants by 7 a.m. This is when the first delivery is made to the West outlet. At least 2 more morning fill-in pastry deliveries are made and, on many days, a fourth late bread delivery in the afternoon.

"We're perhaps best known for the quality of our cream goods," Bill says. "We use only 40% butterfat cream for whipping, no substitutes or extenders. On Thursday, alone, we'll use 30 gal. of cream to make cream pies, whipped

From a cover article in Bakery Production, *1974*

Wendi's fourth birthday party at Queen and Kiddie land in Bloomington. Her birthday cakes were always made by her Zadie Morrie.

competitions and later ran the international business HD Bakery Consulting, based in Minnesota. He has developed many recipes for well-known retail outlets and was kind enough to consult on many of the Lincoln Del recipes collected here.

Daniel fondly remembers the popular Lincoln Del Bakery tours. Many groups of children from the local synagogues and schools were captivated by the smells and sights as they filed past the huge walk-in coolers, crowded with tall carts of rising breads and resting pastry dough. They watched the bakers, clad in stiff black work boots and flour- and butter-stained aprons. The bakers were always happy to see the curious children and their smiles of delight as they watched the bakers load the breads into the big, hot ovens. A dim orange glow illuminated the insides of the ovens as the children hopped up on a bench to look through the small glass window to see the slowly rotating shelves of baking bread.

Daniel walked the children around the bakery to see the large bins of ingredients under the long, sturdy wooden tables. Many types of flour, cornmeal, sugar, salt, nuts, chocolate chips, sesame seeds, and poppy seeds filled the bins. Just past the giant mixers on a long table sat big containers as large as washing machine boxes filled with blocks of shortening and butter. To the right of the huge hunk of butter was a closed dumbwaiter, and the children were told of the rides the baking supplies took from the basement, where they were delivered from the metal doors on the sidewalk in front of the Del. Their faces lit up as Daniel told them of the cement ramps the flour bags slid down into the storage room and how they were piled on a wheelbarrow to make their way to the "elevator" that brought them up to the bakers.

On the long wooden tables that filled the bakery, hungry children decorated sugar cookies and sneaked a few handfuls of chocolate chips as a snack. They also played with bagel dough and made their own shapes. The children took their cookie creations out of the bakery and down the

THE
Lincoln
DEL

Cookie Corner

VALUABLE COUPON
Your Free Cookie!
The bearer of this

Cookie Card

is entitled to one

Free Cookie!

from any Lincoln Del
Kid's Cookie Corner.
Visit Lincoln Del East or South to
redeem this Cookie Card for one

Deeee-licious
Cookie

Remember walking in the front entrance and immediately drooling over these cases? What's wrong with dessert before the meal?

back hallway, past the dishwasher, past the deli case, and into the restaurant to sit at the tables where glasses of milk waited for them. The tours offered one delight after another, and the Del employees were always patient and amused by the kids' reactions. The Lincoln Del Bakery tours were a highly anticipated field trip for kids and teachers alike, creating memories that have lasted for generations.

The true talents behind the Lincoln Del food were head prep chef Edna Dye and Tess Berenberg. Edna and Tess were always energized over a new recipe, and they bounced ingredient ideas back and forth. Tess experimented at home and brought her successes to Edna to reproduce in bulk quantities to see if the flavors translated for restaurant use. Sometimes they savored their creations in Edna's prep kitchen, located in the basement of the Lake Street Del. They opened the door just across from the restrooms and knocked on the always-locked office door to share with the office staff "testers."

Edna was happy to stop for a big hello and a hug even if she was elbow-deep in a vat of potato salad. At the end of her shift, usually after the main dinner crowd came in, Edna stopped by Tess and Morrie's home, samples in tow. All who sat at the Berenbergs' dinner table, sometimes across three generations, got the chance to taste Edna's newest concoctions. They discussed recipes that could use a tweak based on customer comments. Was the borscht too sour? Did the meatballs have enough onions? Was the schmaltz too salty? What about the potato salad? Everyone had a say in the final product. And those "taste memories" have guided the home-use recipes developed for this book.

The Lincoln Del West was the first Lincoln Del to have both a restaurant and a bar. Tess Berenberg's collection of clown oil paintings hung in the bar alongside the swordfish Izzy Berenberg caught in Acapulco. This location

THE LINCOLN DEL *and Me* IN THE MID-1960S

BY JACK ZELKIN

I GRADUATED from the University of Colorado in June 1959. Three days later I was on a train to Lackland Air Force Base to begin boot camp in the Air Force reserves.

On a vacation to Las Vegas with a friend of mine, Stan Brown, we were at the Riviera swimming pool and Stan noticed this girl with a Jewish star around her neck. Stan insisted that I go talk to her, which did not thrill me, but I did it anyway. Her name was Mickey Berenberg. She was sitting near her father. . . . When I approached Mickey to talk to her, her father watched me very closely.

This was the beginning of a new life that included marriage and children. After our wedding in Minneapolis, we lived in Denver as I continued my career as a stockbroker. After our daughter Wendi Lynn was born in Denver, Mickey had just turned twenty-one and was very lonesome for her family. She persuaded me to move to Minneapolis and to begin working for her father Morrie at the Lincoln Del. The next seven years produced our second beautiful daughter, Tammi Lynn, while I went through Lincoln Del Boot Camp Training (this made Air Force basic training seem like preschool).

Lincoln Del Training
Morrie designed my training to include working in every facet of the Del's operations . . . including bakery, dishwasher, busboy, prep kitchen, food service line including egg station, hamburger and steak stations, and salad station. To simplify, I learned to prepare every single item that was on the menu.

I eventually moved to the deli and learned how to be a salami slicer, a lox slicer, a bread slicer. I waited on customers and readied the items fresh from the bakery and prep kitchen for sale. During my deli counter days (and nights), my interaction with Morrie became more frequent as both Morrie and I were in the front of the house with customers.

While I was working behind the deli counter, Morrie would say to me, "Let's talk," and I would come out from behind the counter. We would lean against the deli counter glass while surveying the entire deli and restaurant.

It seemed that Morrie was always plagued with "gastro-eruptions." While leaning against the deli counter and surrounded by customers and his cronies, Morrie was forced to relieve himself of the intestinal gas that caused him distress. The subsequent explosions were heard by all of the people around us . . . of course, they turned to look at us. As the customers and cronies stared at us, Morrie's favorite prank was to turn and look at me with an accusing look on his face. He would laugh, move away from me, and shake his head.

The deli counter was my last position before Morrie thought that I was ready to be a manager. I was promoted to general manager and helped open the second St. Louis Park location, Lincoln Del West. One day I went to Morrie to discuss a problem that I was having. He looked at me and very slowly said, "Hey kid, are you looking for sympathy?"

I said, "Maybe."

He looked at me straight in the eye and said, "Kid, there's only one place around here that you will find sympathy; go grab a dictionary and look between sh*t and syphilis!"

Morrie's genius was his absolute demand for quality. I learned an incredible amount about running a food business and how to relate to customers and employees alike. He taught his cooks and bakers to produce *only top-quality* products. Morrie's Lincoln Del West and his two other locations were and still are recognized around the country as one of the finest deli, bakery, restaurant, and cocktail lounge operations in the United States. The entire family, including Mickey and our daughters, were lucky to be born into and involved in running an amazingly successful business. ℒ

Mouthwatering choices always awaited Lincoln Del customers.

opened with Jack Zelkin, the author's father, at the helm. He started working from the bottom to the top a year after Wendi was born. Zelkin met Morrie Berenberg and his daughter Mickey in Las Vegas while Berenberg attended a baker's convention. Zelkin understood immediately that the family was serious about their product, both in front of the counter and behind it. He recalls the Berenbergs' perfectionist tendencies, as they insisted on only the best ingredients to make all of the menu items.

Zelkin became great friends with head cook Bob Teitelbaum and bartender Howard Sprague, often spending time together with their families at Sprague's lakefront home on Lake Minnetonka. As the owner's son-in-law, it was both a blessing and a curse to work at the Del. The pressure was often difficult, but the time spent in the popular Jewish community institution has never left him. As an outsider from Denver, Zelkin changed his life by marrying the boss's daughter.

The Lincoln Del South was the third and largest restaurant, bakery, deli, and bar, with seating for as many as three hundred people. Morrie and Tess's son Danny Berenberg spent most of his time there, overseeing the operations. The prep kitchens operated out of the south location and supplied menu items to the Del West, which housed the bakery.

Danny hired so many of his friends' children that an entire generation of students from St. Louis Park remembers the Del as their first real job. Sheldon Rhodes says, "He offered my son some part-time work and I said, 'Danny you don't really have this opening,' and he said, 'I'll have him tomorrow. He has to go to school.' He helped my second son, too.

"He never forgot that when he was a boy they didn't have any money, so he tried to provide all these things for the kids." ♥

Celebrations and Commemorations

Let food be thy medicine and medicine be thy food.
HIPPOCRATES

People who love to eat are always the best people.
JULIA CHILD

Well, it was more than a restaurant; it was like a family,
a place where people started coming as children,
with their parents, and then their own children, and ended
up there with their oxygen tanks.
ROLLIE TROUP

STARTING IN THE MID-1960S, much of the local Twin Cities nightlife was centered around the hotels that sprang up along the borders of Highway 494. Customers had a drink at the Del, went dancing at one of the hotels, and then came back for a nightcap at the Del. Later, as more and more office complexes were built, the Del became a center for the lunch crowd. Many of the business owners and company executives who weren't restricted to a formal lunch hour would come to the Del and stay for a couple of hours to conduct business. The Del was a regular stop for travelers arriving or departing at the nearby Minneapolis–St. Paul Airport. While awaiting a flight, hungry customers popped in to purchase bakery and deli items to bring back home or to satisfy a long-remembered craving. Tour buses stopped at the Del as well. For tailgaters at a Vikings game or visitors to the newly built Mall of America, the Del catered events on a large scale. The South Del, with its large prep kitchen and chefs' kitchen, regularly hosted Bloomington-based business celebrations as well as art openings for friends of the Del.

HARRY M

LINCOLN DEL SOUTH

JUNE 11, 1998

A BENEFIT FOR THI

cCORMICK

FINGERHUT GALLERY
JUNE 12 – 13, 1998
CANCER KIDS FUND

PREVIOUS PAGE *Harry McCormick's famous restaurant paintings always depicted actual customers.*

Painter Harry McCormick is known for his elegant interiors, particularly of interesting bars, and also for his portrayals of average folks doing ordinary things. The Berenbergs' large collection of McCormick paintings hung in the bar of the Lincoln Del South. Loyal customer and friend Tom Whelan had a copy of *McSorley's Tavern,* and the Del also had a print. Discussing their mutual interest, Danny Berenberg mentioned to Tom that the next time they were both in New York City they should drink a beer or two at McSorley's on the Lower East Side. The gathering was planned shortly thereafter. In preparation for the trip, Danny called Allan Fingerhut, who had sold the McCormick paintings to the Del, and cajoled Allan into giving him Harry McCormick's telephone number. Danny called Harry and invited him to join the enthusiasts at McSorley's. The artist accepted, and thus began a long friendship among the three men.

As Harry's primary subject matter was bar scenes, always with beautiful women featured prominently, Danny suggested that he might be interested in painting the Lincoln Del South bar, where so many of his works were proudly displayed. They agreed that Harry would travel to Minnesota to photograph the bar in preparation for a painting.

On the way to Lincoln Del South from the Minneapolis–St. Paul Airport, Danny warned Harry that he would likely be descended upon by patrons who had for years seen his paintings hanging in the bar. They would have lots of questions and opinions. And in fact for several days Harry enjoyed celebrity status at the bar, an unusual occurrence for the artist, accustomed to toiling in obscurity.

Harry shot his photos, returned home to New York, and commenced drawing and painting. Months passed, with Harry regularly sending copies of his outtakes. He captured many of the bar patrons, and several personal friends of the family, including Don Little and Darlene Meyer. The Berenbergs, including Danny, his wife Robin, their son Jake, and Tess, were painted in, though not seated at the bar. On Danny's insistence, the artist painted himself in, too. Many bar patrons and staff were impressed by the outtake drawings on craft paper with pen and ink, shipped to Danny for review (some of these still exist in Danny's private collection). Those who objected to Harry's characterization of them were immediately painted out and thereby forever lost to posterity.

Though to Harry a painting is never quite finished, he eventually had the result framed in gold and shipped to Minnesota. The painting remained shrouded pending Harry's arrival for an opening show at the Del, an occasion that was used as a fundraiser for several local charities, including the Kaiser Roll. After the one-day opening at Lincoln Del South, Allan Fingerhut kindly agreed to continue the showing at his Fingerhut Gallery in Edina's Galleria mall.

Danny had asked all Lincoln Del departments to use their particular skills to create ways to enhance the opening. The restaurant division rearranged the entire dining room to accommodate a number of selected paintings that Harry brought in addition to the star of the show. The bar made special rum drinks for the opening, and the bakery created a special bread to commemorate the event.

But Danny wanted to find some thread tying all this creativity to the McCormick painting. He concocted a story—fictional from start to finish—about a nonexistent Captain McCormick. Danny's story went that Harry's family tree included a long-lost ship captain who sailed from London to the Caribbean islands to pick up rum and then to Boston to trade the rum for cod to be transported back to London. On a return leg near Boston, Captain Mac's ship was imperiled in a hurricane. Additionally, there was some question about the crew being impaired due to too much rum. The ship was lost, but the crew and captain made it to shore with many casks of rum. Unable to return to England, the crew turned to the enterprise of baking and selling a special "Captain Mac's" bread, made with rum in addition to sugar. The bread, so the story goes, became famous in Boston, and the formula was discovered by the Lincoln Del bakers, who duplicated it for the opening party. Keep in mind, all of this was total fiction.

Danny printed more than a thousand posters and a hundred giclées, and McCormick signed them for the opening. Many of these still hang at sites around the Twin Cities and as far away as Europe and South America. Entertainment at the opening included performances by Tiny Tim, the Apollo Men's Choir, and a gospel group from North Minneapolis. The collaboration and blending of the three distinct performance styles was spectacular. The opening was well publicized by *Minnesota Monthly* magazine, complete with the Captain Mac story, as well as a broad range of Minneapolis media. Some thousand guests attended the event in Bloomington. Harry brought his wife, Myuki, as well as his two brothers. Danny apologized for making up the story about Captain Mac, but the brothers immediately corrected him, insisting that they knew the tale was actually true. Already it had become a family legend.

Sheldon Rhodes was a customer at the Del South practically every day, from its opening in 1975 until its closing in 2000. He and his friends had a regular table in the mornings. "It was like our country club," he says. "It was just a tremendous place to go. In the morning, you had the same people there day after day. You'd sit down at a table, and somebody would leave and somebody else would take their spot. It was a meeting place. Everybody gathered and told stories. The business community made a lot of connections there. There was usually a line waiting to get in. We used to say that every day was Saturday night."

The regulars came and went, Sheldon says:

We had a table, and you'd sit down and have breakfast, and this guy would stop and that guy would stop. It wasn't necessarily always the same people. You had your little bunch of people you worked with or did business with. There was always somebody there. I'd occasionally have breakfast with the [Bloomington] mayor. We had several mayors of course during the tenure of the Del. And people on the city council. Danny was very involved with the city and promoting the hospitality industry and trying to attract conventions. I'm sure he was involved with promoting the Mall of America. He just had this knack. . . .

Although we were customers at both of the St. Louis Park locations, the Del on 494 and France Avenue in Bloomington became like a second home. I was there the morning it opened and ate there nearly every day in the morning and sometimes for lunch—and many dinners—and this continued until the very last day of food operations. The only time I wasn't there was if I was out of town or sick. If we were having an event in our home, such as birthdays, anniversaries, graduation parties, or holidays, we never thought of calling anywhere else to order food for our guests.

The Del was a place where everybody knew your name. It was like *Cheers*, except we didn't have Cliff or Norm; instead we had Harold, Larry, and Reynolds, who were regulars at lunch at the South Del bar and always sat in the same seats. The South Del started the "Kaiser Roll" race and raised many thousand dollars for charity. Twenty thousand people attended the race annually for many years. National and local TV news crews were on-site, and the Lincoln Del sign was always visible as an excellent advertising source.

Both of our sons worked at the Del part-time while attending school, delivering box lunches to the many offices in the area as well as working the Kaiser Roll events. At one time my wife, Fran, was homebound for a week and every morning at 11 AM she received a phone call from Danny asking what she wanted for lunch, and they delivered the order.

There was always something going on at the Del. It was a gathering place for political people . . . [and] celebrities as well. It was *the* place to go. Everybody would say, "Meet me at the Del." To this day, no one has even come close to an omelette or order of hash browns like the Del served. We miss this restaurant.

Sheldon remembers, "When we were liquidating the Del South, some of the people from the hospitality industry came by. I remember the chef came in from I think it was Kincaid's [Restaurant in St. Paul], and it was the first time he'd ever seen the kitchen—the Del South was huge—and he said, 'My boss would kill for a kitchen like this. What they have here is everything you could ever want and all top quality.'"

Few restaurants today can afford to pay their employees a living wage. Pastry chef Daniel Hemiadan bought his family a house with his salary from the Del. Server Rollie Troup put herself through the University of Minnesota, paying her tuition and living expenses with money she earned as a waitress. You'd never be able to do that now.

Soaring costs and the Del's high standards did not always translate to a workable business vision. The days of employees making the Del their career were dwindling. Expenses related to labor, food, and overall operation of two restaurants led to the decision to close. Unfortunately, goodwill alone could not sustain the business. When the Del closed its doors in 2000, the regulars were devastated. "Where are we going to go now?" they asked. For a while they tried other restaurants, but nothing could match the friendliness—or the food, or the service, or the camaraderie—of the Del. ❦

FRIDAY LUNCHEON MENU

SLIM DIET LUNCH

Clam Chowder 1.55
Chicken Soup with Rice .... 1.45 and 1.95
Matzo Ball Soup .... .75
Chilled Tomato Juice ....

DAILY LUNCH SPECIAL
Cup of Clam Chowder, BAR-B-Q BEEF on
Kaiser Roll, Cole Slaw
$3.95

WIENER SPECIAL—*Soup, Char-Broiled Wiener (1),
Tomato Slice, Choice of Potato Salad, French
Fries or Whipped Potatoes, Rolls and Butter   3.35

HOT ROAST BEEF SANDWICH, Whipped
Potatoes, Natural Gravy 4.25
SPANISH OMELETTE, Rolls and Butter 3.30
*SOUP, CORNED BEEF SANDWICH 3.65
*SOUP, BAR-B-Q BEEF SANDWICH 3.25
BAR-B-Q BEEF SANDWICH on a Bun 2.55

*Chicken — Matzo Ball 45c Extra, Chowder 55c Extra

Tomato Vegetable Soup, Cup 1.00

7 ALBACORE TUNA .. 3.65   SALMON .. 3.85
Tossed Salad, Slim Diet Dressing, String Beans, Bread

8 TURKEY REUBEN (Open Face) 2.85
Melted Cheese and Kraut on Toast

9 BROILED GROUND BEEF 3.45
String Beans, Bread, Tossed Salad, Slim Diet Dressing

10 LEAN ROAST BEEF 4.40
String Beans, Bread, Tossed Salad, Slim Diet Dressing

11 FRESH ROASTED SLICED TURKEY 3.75
White Bread, Tomato Juice

12 FRANKS (2), SAUERKRAUT, Bread 3.95

Beverage Extra — No Substitutions

FRUIT JELLO 1.10

STUFFED TOMATO/EGG or CHICKEN SALAD, Rolls and Butter 3.95
STUFFED TOMATO/ALBACORE TUNA or SALMON SALAD, Rolls and Butter 4.50
MACARONI and TUNA SALAD, Vegetable, Choice of Dressing on Side, Rolls and Butter ... 3.95
HAWAIIAN FRESH FRUIT PLATE, Choice of Cottage Cheese, Sherbert, Whipped Cream, Muffin 4.95

THURSDAY LUNCHEON MENU

Vegetable or Chicken Soup with Noodles 1.00
Matzo Ball Soup .... 1.45 and 1.95
Chilled Tomato Juice .... .75

DAILY LUNCH SPECIAL
Cup of Vegetable *Soup, BAKED MEAT LOAF
on Choice of Bread, Cole Slaw
$3.45

WIENER SPECIAL—*Soup, Char-Broiled Wiener (1),
Tomato Slice, Choice of Potato Salad, French
Fries or Whipped Potatoes, Rolls and Butter   3.35

SPANISH OMELETTE, Rolls and Butter 3.30
HOT ROAST BEEF SANDWICH, Whipped
Potatoes, Natural Gravy 4.25
MEAT LOAF SANDWICH 2.45
*SOUP, CORNED BEEF SANDWICH 3.65
*SOUP, BAR-B-Q BEEF SANDWICH 3.25
BAR-B-Q BEEF SANDWICH on a Bun 2.55

*Vegetable or Chicken — Matzo Ball 45c Extra

SLIM DIET LUNCH

Tomato Vegetable Soup, Cup 1.00

7 ALBACORE TUNA .. 3.65   SALMON .. 3.85
Tossed Salad, Slim Diet Dressing, String Beans, Bread

8 TURKEY REUBEN (Open Face) 2.85
Melted Cheese and Kraut on Toast

9 BROILED GROUND BEEF 3.45
String Beans, Bread, Tossed Salad, Slim Diet Dressing

10 LEAN ROAST BEEF 4.40
String Beans, Bread, Tossed Salad, Slim Diet Dressing

11 FRESH ROASTED SLICED TURKEY 3.75
White Bread, Tomato Juice

12 FRANKS (2), SAUERKRAUT, Bread 3.95

Beverage Extra — No Substitutions

FRUIT JELLO 1.10

STUFFED TOMATO/EGG or CHICKEN SALAD, Rolls and Butter 3.95
STUFFED TOMATO/ALBACORE TUNA or SALMON SALAD, Rolls and Butter 4.50
MACARONI and TUNA SALAD, Vegetable, Choice of Dressing on Side, Rolls and Butter 3.95
HAWAIIAN FRESH FRUIT PLATE, Choice of Cottage Cheese, Sherbert, Whipped Cream, Muffin 4.95

TUESDAY LUNCHEON MENU

Navy Bean Soup or Chicken Soup with Noodles 1.00
Matzo Ball Soup . . . . 1.45 and 1.95
Chilled Tomato Juice 75

DAILY LUNCH SPECIAL

Cup of Navy Bean *Soup, CORNED BEEF and
SWISS CHEESE on Two Pumpernickle Rolls,
Cole Slaw
$3.50

WIENER SPECIAL—*Soup, Char-Broiled Wiener (1),
Tomato Slice, Choice of Potato Salad, French
Fries or Whipped Potatoes, Rolls and Butter 3.35

SPANISH OMELETTE, Rolls and Butter 3.30

HOT ROAST BEEF SANDWICH, Whipped
Potatoes, Natural Gravy 4.25

*SOUP, CORNED BEEF SANDWICH 3.65

*SOUP, BAR-B-Q BEEF SANDWICH 3.25

BAR-B-Q BEEF SANDWICH on a Bun 2.55

*Navy Bean or Chicken — Matzo Ball 45c Extra

SLIM DIET LUNCH

Tomato Vegetable Soup, Cup 1.00

7 ALBACORE TUNA . . 3.65   SALMON . . 3.85
Tossed Salad, Slim Diet Dressing, String Beans, Bread

8 TURKEY REUBEN (Open Face) 2.85
Melted Cheese and Kraut on Toast

9 BROILED GROUND BEEF 3.45
String Beans, Bread, Tossed Salad, Slim Diet Dressing

10 LEAN ROAST BEEF 4.40
String Beans, Bread, Tossed Salad, Slim Diet Dressing

11 FRESH ROASTED SLICED TURKEY 3.75
White Bread, Tomato Juice

12 FRANKS (2), SAUERKRAUT, Bread 3.95

Beverage Extra — No Substitutions

FRUIT JELLO 1.10

STUFFED TOMATO/EGG or CHICKEN SALAD, Rolls and Butter 3.95
STUFFED TOMATO/ALBACORE TUNA or SALMON SALAD, Rolls and Butter 4.50
MACARONI and TUNA SALAD, Vegetable, Choice of Dressing on Side, Rolls and Butter 3.95
HA . . . . FRUIT PLATE, Choice of Cottage Cheese, Sherbert, Whipped Cream, Muffin 4.95

WEDNESDAY DINNER MENU

DINNER SERVED 5:00 P.M. TO 9:00 P.M.
(ALA CARTE DINNERS INCLUDE HOT BREAD)

Soup of the day — BEEF BARLEY/DUMPLING . . 1.00

BRAISED BEEF TENDERLOIN TIPS
Potato 6.45
          Ala Carte . . 4.95

SWEET and SOUR MEAT BALLS
Choice of Potato or Knish 6.95
          Ala Carte . . 5.45

SAUTEED CHICKEN LIVERS, Potato
Mushrooms and Onions 6.45
          Ala Carte . . 4.95

U.S. CHOICE SIRLOIN of ROAST BEEF au Jus
Potato 7.45
          Ala Carte . . 5.95

GRILLED SALMON or BROILED HALIBUT
Melted Butter, Potato 7.45
          Ala Carte . . 5.95

THE ABOVE DINNERS INCLUDE: Beef Barley Soup with
Dumpling, Chicken Soup with Rice, Matzo Ball or Chilled
Tomato Juice, Salad Bowl, Choice of Potato, Hot Bread.
Beverage Extra

FEATURE

Hot Beef Sandwich
Mashed Potatoes, au Jus 4.50

SLIM DIET MENU

Tomato Vegetable Soup, Cup 1.00
13 Lean Roast Beef 7.45
14 Fresh Roasted Sliced Turkey (cold) 6.75
15 Franks (2) and Sauerkraut 6.75
16 Lean Broiled Ground Beef 5.00
17 Fancy Red Alaska Salmon (cold) . . 7.45
18 Broiled Halibut Steak 7.45

SERVED WITH THE ABOVE—Tomato Juice or Cup of
Beef or Chicken Bouillon, Tossed Salad, Slim Diet
Dressing, Cooked Vegetable of the Day, Jello.
Beverage Extra

Fruit Jello 1.10

★ ★ ★ ★ ★   **OTHER SUGGESTIONS**   ★ ★ ★ ★ ★

STUFFED TOMATO/Egg or Chicken Salad, Hot Bread
STUFFED TOMATO/Albacore Tuna or Salmon Salad, Hot Bread
FRIED CHICKEN (1/2), Potato, Slaw or Salad, Hot Bread 3.95
FILET of WALLEYE PIKE, Potato, Slaw or Salad, Hot Bread 4.50
FRENCH FRIED SHRIMP (6), Potato, Tartar Sauce, Hot Bread 5.95
CHICKEN & RIBS, Potato, Slaw or Salad, Hot Bread 6.95
STEAK PLATTER, 8 oz. Choice Tenderloin served on Toast, Potato, Slaw or Salad 7.95
BAR-B-RIBS, Special Sauces, Potato, Toast, Slaw or Salad (HALF ORDER RIBS 8.95

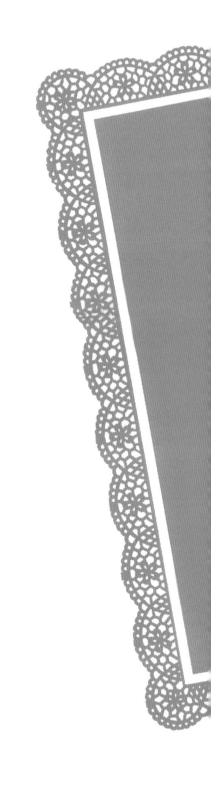

THE
Recipes

DISCLAIMER

THE AUTHORS have made every effort to convert treasured Del recipes from restaurant quantities to those more suitable for the home cook. While instructions are similar to those used at the Del, some ingredients may be difficult to find. We've shopped at local grocery stores or gone to places like Walmart and Amazon.com for such items as pumpernickel rye flour, sour salt, high-ratio shortening (also called "cake shortening"), or whipped cream stabilizer. In our original large-batch recipes, shortening was a more economical choice over butter. Of course, you are free to use butter instead for even more wonderful flavor. Individual cooking abilities could affect the outcome of the recipes, and there's no accounting for nostalgia (no taste can match the deliciousness of our memories). Commercial ovens tend to bake hotter and with a more uniform temperature than residential ovens do. Still, we hope you are able to re-create, if not the actual dishes, the sense of love and community we felt at the Del. The Berenberg family retains copyright of all recipes. We hope you have a wonderful time with our recipes in your kitchen.

Breakfast

OMELETTE

SECRETS TO MAKING A GREAT SOUFFLE OMELETTE

The Lincoln Del's famous Cheese Omelette is the most requested recipe next to the Chocolate Pie (page 108). It is the one item that still makes people swoon and prompts them to ask anyone within hearing, "Have you eaten the Del omelette? Oh my, it looked and tasted amazing!" This puffy delight was made of three jumbo eggs whipped, then lightly cooked in a pan with clarified butter; additional ingredients were added to the half-cooked eggs as they just barely took shape in the pan; then the omelette was folded over ever so gently into an individual oval baking dish and baked in a high-temperature oven with slices of cheese or other requested items draped atop. An omelette masterpiece not unlike a soufflé, the result was gently spooned out of the baking dish in one large piece at the table in front of the wide-eyed, hungry customer.

"It's all in the wrist." Chef Jimmy Johnson supervises an omelette class.

The Cheese Omelette tasted amazing all by itself, but the adventurous eater could add just about anything to it for a complete meal. Some ate the omelette as a Sunday-morning ritual; some had it for dinner because it was just that good whatever the time of day. Wendi used the omelette as a special test for all her dates. Her future husband passed the most difficult hurdle of watching her devour a well-done liver and onions omelette on his first visit to the Del. He looked a bit frightened at the enormity of the puffy omelette as it was served. He certainly had reservations about kissing her after the meal.

Here are some tips for re-creating this wonder in your own kitchen:

→ The longer you whip the eggs, the fluffier the omelette.

→ Use a cast-iron or aluminum pan. Teflon or nonstick pans are okay, but they do not heat as evenly.

→ Practice your flipping technique with a piece of toast. Remember: it's all in the wrist. (You can always use a spatula to fold it over in the pan instead of flipping it.)

→ When you transfer the omelette to the baking pan, the eggs should be still runny in the center and very hot: their heat helps the omelette to rise in the oven.

METHOD

Preheat oven to 375 degrees. Use a blender to thoroughly whip 3 jumbo eggs. Preheat the skillet. When the pan is warm, add a tablespoon of clarified butter. Allow butter to get hot before adding whipped eggs, but watch carefully so it doesn't burn.

Gently pour whipped eggs into pan, being careful not to coat the sides. Stir with a fork while gently shaking the pan to prevent burning. When the omelette seems set on the bottom, spread on your toppings (except for cheese; see below). Then it's time to flip. Be gentle; don't go too high. After several flips, add cheese to the middle, then immediately fold omelette in half and transfer to an ovensafe omelette dish. Place additional cheese on top.

Bake until golden, about 5 minutes.

OTHER INGREDIENTS

Use your favorite cheese, but beware of pepper cheese: it tends to burn and discolor. Anything you add to your omelette should be precooked and kept hot. The more ingredients you add, the harder it will be to handle.

For Denver mix, add chopped corned beef, green bell peppers, and onions. Other favorite additions are fried chicken livers and onions, salmon and cream cheese, and even jelly.

CORNED BEEF HASH

¼–½ pound medium-fat corned beef, chopped into
    bite-size pieces

2 tablespoons canola oil

1 large onion, chopped

4 large baking potatoes, cooked, peeled, and chopped

salt and pepper

1 egg, beaten

YIELD: 4 EXTRA-LARGE SERVINGS
Everybody gets hungry for this dish, amazing to eat anytime, 24/7.

Wrap the sliced corned beef in foil and place in a 350-degree oven to warm for 5 minutes. Preheat 8-inch skillet over high heat, then add canola oil, onions, and potatoes. Season to taste with salt and pepper. Cook potatoes until crispy on the bottom and sides. Add the warmed corned beef and beaten egg to the pan and mix well. Flip the hash to brown the other side. Remove from heat, slip hash into an aluminum pie pan, place upside down on a plate, and use paper towel to press out any excess oil before serving.

GOLDEN HASH BROWNS

2 tablespoons clarified butter

6 medium baking potatoes, peeled, shredded, and
    squeezed dry

salt and pepper

chopped onions, optional

chopped peppers, optional

YIELD: 4 LARGE SERVINGS
While our famous Corned Beef Hash (above) uses canola oil, this recipe calls for clarified butter, the best choice for high-heat cooking.

Preheat 8-inch skillet over high heat; add butter and then shredded potatoes; season with salt and pepper. Stir to allow bottom and top to cook to a golden color. Stir in onions and peppers, if using. When potatoes are crispy, flip into an aluminum pie pan, slide onto a plate, and use paper towel to press out any excess butter before serving. Adjust seasoning to taste.

FRENCH TOAST

2 large eggs

¼ cup milk

2 (1½-inch) slices Challah (page 147)

2 tablespoons clarified butter (see note page 103)

confectioner's sugar for topping

Stir together eggs and milk until well blended. Thoroughly soak bread slices in egg mixture. On preheated griddle or in preheated skillet, melt clarified butter and then cook bread on each side until golden brown, about 5 minutes total. Serve with confectioner's sugar sprinkled on top.

YIELD: 1 SERVING

Customers waiting for a seat could see this delicious, thick-sliced, any-time-of-day dish from across the restaurant. The most decadent version uses fresh challah bread and is smothered with butter and syrup . . . and fresh fruit for the guilty few who want a slightly healthier option.

HOMEMADE PANCAKE SYRUP

7 small pots granulated sugar

3 small pots packed brown sugar

6 small pots boiling water

2 gallons dark corn syrup

½ cup imitation maple flavoring

Combine sugars, mixing well. Pour boiling water over mixed sugar. Stir in corn syrup and maple flavoring.

YIELD: 6 GALLONS

How could we not include this recipe? It's in bulk restaurant amounts, which makes sharing this method even more delightful. A "small pot" equals 6 cups.

WILD BLUEBERRY MUFFINS

2¼ cups cake flour, plus more for dusting

1 tablespoon baking powder

¼ teaspoon salt

1 cup shortening (see note) or butter, softened

1 cup sugar

8 large eggs

1 cup evaporated milk

3 cups blueberries, preferably fresh; if frozen, thawed, drained, and patted dry

1 tablespoon cinnamon

pinch lemon zest

YIELD:
4 DOZEN MUFFINS;
RECIPE CAN BE HALVED

This recipe, one of the first Wendi tested, did not disappoint. The taste memory was immediate. Made with shortening, it truly duplicated the flavor of the freshly baked muffin straight from the Del's oven. Of course, the next bake had to include butter to create a rich, decadent flavor that highlighted the fresh blueberries. Delicious!

Preheat oven to 425 degrees. Prepare muffin pans with papers or nonstick spray. In a small bowl, whisk together flour, baking powder, and salt. In bowl of stand mixer, combine shortening and sugar and beat until light and fluffy. Beat in eggs and evaporated milk. Gradually add flour mixture, beating just to combine.

Dust blueberries with a tablespoon of flour and cinnamon, toss with lemon zest, and stir in to mix. Divide batter into muffin pans, filling each compartment ⅔ full. Bake until the muffins rise, about 10 minutes, then reduce heat to 375 degrees and continue baking for another 10 minutes, until golden brown.

NOTE: The original recipe calls for "high-ratio shortening," which, with more emulsifiers than vegetable shortening, can absorb more liquid without breaking down. It's hard to find these days, but you can order it from Cake Central (http://cakecentral.com/). It's also available at Amazon.com.

BRAN MUFFINS

YIELD: 12 LARGE MUFFINS

Crushed pineapple makes these muffins remarkably sweet. This breakfast staple is amazing when toasted.

1¾ cups bran

1½ cups all-purpose flour

1 tablespoon baking soda

1 teaspoon salt

1 cup plus 3 tablespoons sugar

¼ cup oil

1 tablespoon butter, softened

1 large egg

1½ cups milk

1 cup crushed pineapple, drained

Preheat oven to 375 degrees. Prepare muffin pans with papers or nonstick spray. In a small bowl, whisk together bran, flour, baking soda, and salt. In bowl of stand mixer, combine sugar, oil, and butter and blend on medium speed. Slowly add egg and milk and continue mixing on medium speed for 4 minutes. On low speed, add flour mixture until just combined. Add pineapple and blend well. Divide batter evenly among muffin compartments. Bake for 25 minutes, until golden brown.

KMISH BREAD

YIELD: 4 LOAVES

This recipe, favored by all, originated in the Berenberg family kitchen. Not too dry, it's sugary goodness. It also freezes well.

2 cups cake flour

2 teaspoons baking powder

½ teaspoon salt

2 teaspoons cinnamon

16 tablespoons (2 sticks) butter, softened

2 cups sugar, plus more for sprinkling

6 large eggs

1 teaspoon vanilla

1 cup chopped nuts

1 cup fruit jam and/or chocolate chips

Preheat oven to 350 degrees. Grease 2 (9x13-inch) glass baking dishes. In a small bowl, whisk together flour, baking powder, salt, and cinnamon. In bowl of stand mixer, beat the butter at medium speed and then add sugar, eggs, and vanilla and blend until smooth. Reduce speed to low and add flour mixture, blending until well mixed. Stir in nuts. Divide dough into 4 equal pieces.

On a large sheet of waxed paper dusted with flour, roll 1 portion of dough to 10 inches wide and 12 inches long. Spread ¼ of the jam and other desired fillings to cover the dough. Use the waxed paper to lift one 12-inch end of the dough and roll it over twice. Place rolled-up dough in pan. Repeat with the remaining ingredients, placing two breads side by side in each pan. Sprinkle loaves with sugar. Bake for 30 to 40 minutes or until lightly golden.

Kmish Bread. Photo by Sam Stern

SOUR CREAM LOAF

8 tablespoons (1 stick) butter, softened

3 cups packed brown sugar

1 tablespoon cinnamon

4 cups all-purpose flour

2 teaspoons baking soda

2 teaspoons baking powder

½ teaspoon salt

1 cup shortening

2 cups granulated sugar

4 large eggs

2 cups sour cream

2 teaspoons vanilla

YIELD: 2 LOAVES
A favorite of Tess and Morrie's grandson Jake. Double the brown sugar mixture that marbles the sweet treat for an extra flavor punch.

Preheat oven to 350 degrees. Grease and lightly flour 2 (9x5-inch) loaf pans. In a large bowl, combine butter, brown sugar, and cinnamon for filling, mixing well. Set filling aside. Combine flour, baking soda, baking powder, and salt and sift together 4 times. In bowl of stand mixer, combine shortening and granulated sugar; beat until smooth. Add eggs, sour cream, and vanilla and blend on medium speed. Reduce to low speed and add flour mixture. Pour ¼ of the batter into each pan, then add ¼ of the filling mixture to each pan. Pour remaining batter evenly in each pan. Top each with remaining filling. Bake for 1 hour.

BANANA BREAD

3 cups all-purpose flour

1 tablespoon baking powder

1 tablespoon baking soda

1 teaspoon salt

1½ cups mashed ripened bananas (about 3 large bananas)

½ cup oil

YIELD: 3 LOAVES
Who can resist banana bread? We have even been known to make french toast with it.

1 cup plus 2 tablespoons sugar

5 large eggs

¼ cup water

¾ cup walnut pieces, optional

Preheat oven to 350 degrees. Grease 3 (8½ x 4½-inch) loaf pans. In a small bowl, whisk together flour, baking powder, baking soda, and salt. In bowl of stand mixer, combine bananas, oil, and sugar. Beat in eggs, one at a time, then water, and blend on medium speed until smooth. Stir in flour mixture, then nuts, if using. Divide batter among prepared pans. Bake for 30 to 35 minutes or until golden brown.

CINNAMON ROLLS AND CARAMEL ROLLS

FOR SWEET DOUGH

5¾ cups all-purpose flour

¾ cup sugar

1 packet (2¼ teaspoons) instant or rapid-rise yeast

2 tablespoons powdered milk

1½ teaspoons salt

¾ cup warm water (110–115 degrees)

¾ cup warmed milk

5 large eggs

FOR CINNAMON ROLLS

2 cups sugar, plus more for sprinkling

1 tablespoon cinnamon

¾ cup (1½ sticks) butter, melted

FOR CARAMEL ROLLS

1¾ cups granulated sugar

1 cup packed brown sugar

1 tablespoon powdered milk

1½ teaspoons salt ⟹

YIELD: 12 ROLLS
These buttery sweet rolls are the perfect addition to any coffee break. Or serve them warm with a glass of cold milk.

¾ cup shortening or butter, softened

⅓ cup honey

2½ tablespoons hot water

In bowl of stand mixer, combine sweet dough ingredients and blend on medium speed for 6 minutes. Let dough rest, covered, for 3 hours in the refrigerator. Proof dough, covered, in 200-degree oven for 45 minutes or until doubled in size. Dough should reach 80 degrees (use an instant-read thermometer).

Preheat oven to 350 degrees. Grease a 7x11-inch baking dish.

FOR CINNAMON ROLLS

On a floured work surface, roll dough into an 8x20-inch rectangle about ¼-inch thick and cover with sugar and cinnamon. Roll up dough, cut into 2-inch-thick slices, and place cut side up in prepared baking dish. Brush rolls with melted butter and sprinkle lightly with sugar. Bake for 10 to 15 minutes, until golden brown.

FOR CARAMEL ROLLS

Blend caramel ingredients on medium speed for 6 minutes. Transfer mixture to a saucepan and warm to a spreadable consistency. Use to fill and top dough as directed above. Prepare and bake rolls as above.

Spread rolls with White Glaze Icing (page 79) if desired.

RAISED YEAST DONUTS

4½ cups all-purpose flour

5 teaspoons instant or rapid-rise yeast

3 tablespoons powdered milk

2½ tablespoons baking powder

2 tablespoons sugar

1½ teaspoons salt

2 large eggs

YIELD: 6 LARGE DONUTS

Go ahead and play with this recipe, adding chocolate chips and other delights.

1¼ cups warm water (110–115 degrees)
½ cup shortening
1½ teaspoons vanilla
3 cups oil for frying
sugar or White Glaze Icing (recipe follows) for rolling

In bowl of stand mixer, combine flour, yeast, powdered milk, baking powder, sugar, salt, eggs, water, shortening, and vanilla, blending on medium speed for 5 to 6 minutes. Cover bowl with plastic wrap and place in a 200-degree proofing oven or other warm place; allow dough to rise and reach 80 degrees (use an instant-read thermometer), approximately 1 hour. Then allow raised dough to rest at room temperature, covered, for 1½ hours. Portion dough, roll into ropes, and shape into donuts ½ inch thick. Place each donut on a parchment paper-lined baking sheet.

In a skillet, heat oil to 375 degrees. Working in batches, fry donuts for 2 minutes on each side. Remove to a cooling rack set over a paper-lined baking sheet to catch dripping oil. When cool enough to handle, roll each donut in sugar or glaze.

WHITE GLAZE ICING

YIELD: 1 CUP

2 cups confectioner's sugar
2 tablespoons butter, softened
1 teaspoon vanilla
1 tablespoon milk

Combine confectioner's sugar, butter, and vanilla in a small saucepan set over medium heat. After the butter has melted, slowly stir in the milk to make a thick glaze. Spread immediately onto cinnamon rolls or donuts.

CHICKEN SOUP *Del-A-Gram*

IN THE WINTER OF 1988–89, the Lincoln Del launched the Chicken Soup Del-A-Gram, with delivery anywhere in the Twin Cities metro area. The concept? A pint of the Del's famous soup, from a recipe passed down through three generations, would be shipped hot by express taxi in a special collector's bowl. The Del-A-Gram cost only $9.95 plus taxi fare, and recipients got to keep the bowl.

Danny Berenberg said, "Let's say a friend or family member gets a cold this winter. What can you send to cheer them up? Flowers are too sentimental; boxes of chocolate make them fat; get-well cards are clichés. But home delivery of authentic Lincoln Del chicken matzoh ball soup? Oy, that's heaven!"

He added, "Under federal health regulations we absolutely cannot claim that a delivery of Lincoln Del chicken soup will cure the Minnesota flu or cold . . . but we're not denying it, either." *L*

EVENING DINNERS

Chicken Soup with Matzo Ball,   Chicken Rice Soup,
Green Split Pea Soup   or   Chilled Tomato Juice
Salad, Choice of Potatoes, Vegetable, Rolls & Butter, Coffee, Tea or Milk   1.90

VIRGINIA BAKED HAM, Pineapple Sauce   2.25

BROILED VEAL CHOPS, Apple Sauce

BRAISED SHORT RIBS with KASHA

GROUND SIRLOIN STEAK (8 oz.)

Soups and Salads

MATZO BALL SOUP

This recipe calls for the signature schmaltz, and the balls can be doctored with a chunk of fresh carrot in the middle to surprise the kids. We recommend chilling the raw matzo ball "dough" for an hour to make it easy to roll the balls and drop them in the boiling chicken broth.

The Del took a basic chicken soup base and added onions, celery, and carrots. At home, the base is eliminated. In a stockpot, combine a parsnip, onions, celery, carrots, ¼ cup fresh chopped dill, and a whole chicken. Add 2 cups chicken broth (optional) and enough water to cover. Cook the soup until the meat falls from the bones, remove the bones, season broth with salt and pepper to taste. About 30 to 45 minutes before serving, drop the matzo balls into the slowly boiling broth to absorb all of the flavors.

The Del's matzo balls were baseball size when dropped into the soup. Oy!

YIELD: 8 SERVINGS

Ask anyone, "What is Jewish food?" and matzo ball soup will be at the top of the list. The quality of the matzo ball soup can literally make or break a new deli. If the matzo balls are too dense, too small, too cold, tasteless, or falling apart, the rest of the menu offerings are suspect. Perfecting the matzo ball is the topic of culinary legend.

MATZO BALL MIX

4 large eggs
1 cup liquefied schmaltz
2–3 cups matzo meal

In bowl of stand mixer, beat eggs on high. Reduce mixer speed and add in schmaltz and matzo. Mix until matzo is well coated and dough is a little sticky. Refrigerate, covered, for at least an hour.   ⟹

Prepare favorite chicken soup or follow instructions on page 81. Form baseball-size matzo balls and gently drop into the boiling broth. Return broth to boiling, then reduce to simmer. The balls should eventually rise to the top. Cook for about 45 minutes, until the ball is cooked to the center. Enjoy!!

BEEF BARLEY SOUP WITH DUMPLINGS

SOUP

2 tablespoons vegetable oil

1½ pounds boneless short ribs

10 cups water

4 cups unsalted beef broth

1 tablespoon beef soup base

2 cups chopped carrots

3 cups chopped onion

3 cups chopped mushrooms

4 cups cooked barley

½ teaspoon salt

½ teaspoon pepper

DUMPLINGS

1½ cups all-purpose flour

2 teaspoons baking powder

½ teaspoon salt

3 tablespoons shortening

1 teaspoon schmaltz

¾ cup water

YIELD: 4 GENEROUS SERVINGS

Introduced to this dish in Baubie Tess's kitchen, Wendi considers this thick, tasty soup to be a meal in itself. Even though it was offered on the Del's menu only two days a week, it was available anytime in the deli freezer cases.

In a stockpot over high heat, warm oil and brown short ribs. Add water, beef broth, and beef base and bring to boil; add vegetables, reduce heat, and simmer until softened and meat is cooked through, up to 2 hours.

For dumplings, in a medium bowl, mix flour, baking powder, and salt. Blend in the shortening until mixture is the texture of fine crumbs. Add schmaltz and water and mix well. Drop tablespoon-size portions into boiling soup. Cook uncovered for 10 minutes; reduce heat and simmer for 10 minutes. Stir in barley and heat through. Season with salt and pepper.

SPLIT PEA WITH HOT DOGS SOUP

2 tablespoons olive oil

2 ribs celery, chopped

½ cup shredded carrots

salt and pepper

2 ham bones or hocks

1 cup sliced hot dogs

2 cups dried green split peas, picked over and rinsed

1 tablespoon ham soup base

8 cups water

YIELD: 6 SERVINGS

Can you ever have enough hot dogs in this soup? We think not. Our favorite option was thickly sliced kosher Hebrew National knockwurst.

Heat oil in a large pot over medium heat. Add celery and carrots, season with salt and pepper, and cook, stirring occasionally, until vegetables are soft, approximately 10 minutes. Stir in ham bones or hocks, hot dogs, split peas, ham base, and water. Bring to a boil, reduce heat, and simmer, uncovered, until peas are very soft, 1½ to 2 hours. Remove ham hocks or bones from soup; strip any meat and add to soup. Season with salt and pepper, and serve.

WEIGHT WATCHERS VEGETABLE SOUP

Back in the early 1960s, the Weight Watchers company, then based in Minnesota, approached the Lincoln Del to develop a few recipes for their customers, also giving us permission to include those recipes in our menu offerings. As you might imagine, the first recipes were not very exciting, using only onions, celery, green bell peppers, mushrooms, bean sprouts, and tomatoes for flavor, but over time, creative and tasty additions were made to the soup.

YIELD: 4 (1-CUP) SERVINGS

We recommend fresh vegetables rather than the canned that were used in bulk at the Del.

½ cup thinly sliced carrot

½ onion, chopped

2 cloves garlic, minced

3 cups fat-free vegetable, chicken, or beef broth

1½ cups cubed green cabbage   ⟹

1 rib celery, chopped

1 green bell pepper, chopped

1 (14-ounce) can French-style green beans, low salt if possible

1 (4-ounce) can mushrooms including juice

½ cup fresh bean sprouts

2 cups tomato purée

1¼ cups water

1 tablespoon tomato paste

2 packets Truvia or other sweetener

½ teaspoon basil

¼ teaspoon oregano

½ teaspoon salt

½ teaspoon pepper

½ cup cubed zucchini

In a stockpot set over low heat, cook carrots, onion, and garlic, stirring occasionally, until softened, about 5 minutes. Add broth and remaining ingredients except zucchini. Bring to a boil, reduce heat, and simmer, covered, for 15 minutes. Stir in zucchini and cook over medium heat for 3 to 4 minutes, until softened.

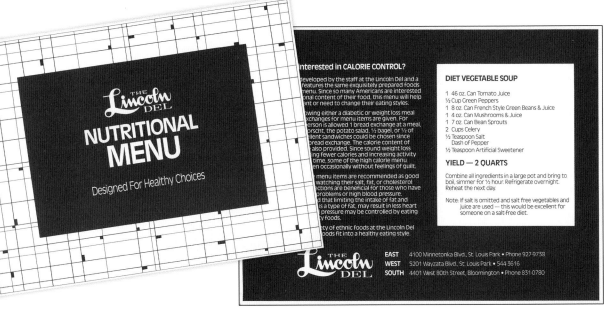

The Lincoln Del shared nutritional information before the practice was commonplace.

WEIGHT WATCHERS SALAD DRESSING

2½ cups condensed tomato juice

2 cups cider vinegar

1½ tablespoons garlic juice

2 tablespoons salt

1½ tablespoons dried onions

1½ tablespoons Truvia or other sweetener

1½ tablespoons Worcestershire sauce

Combine all ingredients, mix well, and refrigerate.

YIELD: ABOUT 5 CUPS

The Del was one of the first restaurants given permission by Weight Watchers to collaborate on and produce their recipes for its customers. When told of the plans for a Lincoln Del cookbook, good friend Cindy Held Tarshish insisted we include this recipe along with the Weight Watchers Vegetable Soup (page 83).

The Lincoln Del
PROUDLY PRESENTS THE
NUTRITIONAL MENU

BREAKFAST

	CALORIES PER SERVING
Cheese Omelette 5 Meat, 9 Fat	740
Wheat Cakes 3 Bread, ½ Milk, 5 Fat	509
Blueberry Pancakes 3 Bread, ½ Fruit, ½ Milk, 5 Fat	528
Topping 1 Fruit	40
Eggs, Lox and Onions 4 Meat, 3 Fat, 1 Vegetable	405
Spanish Omelet 3 Meat, 2 Vegetables, 5 Fat	494
Matzo and Eggs 1½ Bread, 2 Meat, 3 Fat	370
Egg Fluff 4 Bread, 1 Fruit, 1 Meat, ½ Fat	403
Fried Egg 1 Meat, 3 Fat	203
Bagel, 1 Whole 3 Bread	186

NUTRITIONAL FAVORITES

	CALORIES PER SERVING
Lo-Cal Diet Lunch 1½ Bread, 1 Vegetable, 4 Meat LOW IN SALT, FAT & CHOLESTEROL	350
Diet Tomato Vegetable Soup — Cup 1 Vegetable	35
Albacore Tuna 1½ Bread, 5 Meat, 2 Vegetables LOW IN FAT & CHOLESTEROL	512
Turkey Melt 1½ Bread, 5 Meat, 1 Vegetable, 1 Fat	563
Salmon 1½ Bread, 5 Meat, 2 Vegetables LOW IN FAT & CHOLESTEROL	502
Broiled Ground Beef 1½ Bread, 6 Meat, 2 Vegetables LOW IN SALT, FAT & CHOLESTEROL	580
Lean Roast Beef 1½ Bread, 4 Meat, 2 Vegetables LOW IN SALT, FAT & CHOLESTEROL	444

FOUNTAIN

	CALORIES PER SERVING
Baked Apple 2 Fruit LOW IN SALT, FAT & CHOLESTEROL	88
Selection of Fresh Fruit 1-2 Fruit LOW IN SALT, FAT & CHOLESTEROL	60-100
Bread Pudding 2 Bread, 2½ Fruit, 1 Milk	430

SANDWICHES

	CALORIES PER SERVING
Corn Beef 2 Bread, 4 Meat, 4 Fat	555
Pastrami 2 Bread, 4 Meat, 1 Fat	435
Tongue 2 Bread, 4 Meat	415
Grilled Cheese 2 Bread, 3 Meat, 6 Fat	610
Roast Beef 2 Bread, 4 Meat LOW IN SALT, FAT & CHOLESTEROL	390
Ham 2 Bread, 4 Meat LOW IN FAT & CHOLESTEROL	407
Hamburger 2 Bread, 4 Meat LOW IN SALT, FAT & CHOLESTEROL	400
Hamburger with Cheese 2 Bread, 5 Meat, 1 Fat	510
Knockwurst 2 Bread, 3 Meat, 3 Fat	325
Salami or Bologna with Egg 2 Bread, 4 Meat, 6 Fat	598
Turkey with Lettuce and Mayonnaise 2 Bread, 4 Meat, 7 Fat	680
Tuna Salad 2 Bread, 4 Meat, 2 Fat	560
Chicken Salad 2 Bread, 1 Vegetable, 2 Meat, 4 Fat	482
Egg Salad 2 Bread, 2 Meat, 4 Fat	460
Fried Egg 2 Bread, 2 Meat, 3 Fat	407
Fried Egg with Bacon 2 Bread, 2 Meat, 6 Fat	542
Lox and Cream Cheese 2 Bread, 2 Meat, 4 Fat	452

TASTY SALADS

	CALORIES PER SERVING
Chef's Salad 7 Meat, 2 Vegetables	536
Dressing 5 Fat	225
Rolls and Butter 2 Bread, 2 Fat	216
Washington Salad 4 Meat, 2 Vegetables, 1 Fat (includes dressing)	377

SPECIALTIES

	CALORIES PER SERVING
Cabbage Borscht — Cup 1 Bread, 1 Vegetable, ½ Meat LOW IN FAT	127
Cabbage Borscht — Bowl 1 Bread, 2 Vegetables, ½ Meat, ½ Fat	170
Potato Pancakes (5) 2 Bread, 1 Meat, 6 Fat	470
Cheese Blintzes (2) 2½ Bread, 1 Meat, 8 Fat	598
Topping 5 Fruit, 2 Fat	290
Cheese Bagliach (2) 2½ Bread, 1 Meat, 2 Fat	328
Topping 5 Fruit, 2 Fat	290
Chicken Matzo Ball Soup — Cup 1½ Bread, 1 Meat, 1 Fat, ½ Vegetable	230
Chicken Matzo Ball Soup — Bowl 3 Bread, 2 Meat, 2 Fat, ½ Vegetable	445

APPETIZERS

	CALORIES PER SERVING
Gefilte Fish 4 Meat LOW IN FAT & CHOLESTEROL	160
Smoked Fish 4 Meat LOW IN FAT & CHOLESTEROL	160
Beet Borscht 1 Vegetable LOW IN FAT & CHOLESTEROL	35
Sour Cream Topping 3 Fat	135

SIDE ORDERS

	CALORIES PER SERVING
Potato Salad 1 Bread, 1 Vegetable, 3 Fat	228
Cabbage Salad 1 Vegetable, 3 Fat	165
Pickled Beets 1 Vegetable, 2 Fruit LOW IN FAT & CHOLESTEROL	110
Combination Salad 2 Vegetables LOW IN SALT, FAT & CHOLESTEROL	52
Diet Dressing ½ Vegetable LOW IN FAT & CHOLESTEROL	16

THOUSAND ISLAND DRESSING

YIELD: 3 CUPS

This recipe popped up in November 2003. As part of the research for the book *Minnesota Eats Out*, Kathryn Strand Koutsky and Linda Koutsky tracked down recipes from the state's legacy restaurants. "[Lincoln Del owner Danny Berenberg] provided the recipe of his mother, Theresa, which was used at the Del, in several locations," wrote Peg Meier for the *Star Tribune*. "There's a quart of the Del's beet borscht added to 4 gallons of salad dressing. For the home version, canned beet borscht or canned diced beets can be substituted. To retain a chunky texture for the dressing, the ingredients are mashed together rather than blended."

2 cups Miracle Whip
½ cup chili sauce
¾ teaspoon Worcestershire sauce
½ cup prepared beet borscht or canned diced beets with juice
2 large hard-cooked eggs, sliced
¼ cup finely chopped green bell pepper

To a medium bowl, add Miracle Whip, chili sauce, Worcestershire sauce, beet borscht, eggs, and green pepper. Use a potato masher to combine the ingredients until well mixed to a chunky texture.

CHOPPED LIVER

1 cup liquefied schmaltz, divided (see note)

3 medium onions, chopped

3 pounds calf liver, deveined, cooked in salted boiling water, and chopped

8 large hard-cooked eggs, peeled

1 teaspoon salt

1 teaspoon pepper

YIELD: 12 SERVINGS

Wendi judges a good deli by the quality of their chopped liver. When she helped Baubie Tess make this recipe at home, she loved smashing the liver, onions, and egg into the grinder.

Warm ½ cup schmaltz over low heat and slowly cook the onions until deeply browned and dry. Remove from heat and let cool.

Using a stand mixer fitted with the grinder attachment, grind half the liver, half the caramelized onions, and 4 eggs; repeat with remaining liver, onions, and eggs. Add most of the remaining schmaltz and then mix until all ingredients are well combined. Add salt and pepper to taste. Place mixture in a round bowl or mold, cover tightly with plastic wrap, and refrigerate for 8 hours or overnight.

NOTE: Found in the freezer section of most grocery stores, schmaltz is made from chicken fat cooked with onions until the onions are soft and browned; then the mixture is cooled and blended in a food processor. The Del's bulk recipe called for 30 pounds of chicken fat and 13 pounds of onions to render 22 pounds of schmaltz. See also *The Book of Schmaltz: Love Song to a Forgotten Fat* by Michael Ruhlman.

CHICKEN SALAD

1 (12-pound) roasted turkey, deboned, meat cut into small cubes

1 large head celery, minced

1–2 cups Miracle Whip

YIELD: 8 GENEROUS SERVINGS

Yes, it's true. It was actually turkey salad.

Combine all ingredients, mix well, and refrigerate.

LINCOLN DEL EGG SALAD AND TUNA SALAD

EGG SALAD

18 hard-cooked eggs, peeled and chopped

1 teaspoon salt

2 cups Miracle Whip

Combine all ingredients; mix well and refrigerate.

TUNA SALAD

4 (6-ounce) cans tuna in water, drained

1 rib celery, minced

1 large hard-cooked egg, chopped

1 cup Miracle Whip

Combine all ingredients, mix well, and refrigerate.

YIELD: 4-6 SERVINGS

A worthy addition to everyone's fridge and best used in sandwiches, tuna melts, or stuffed tomatoes—or enjoyed by the spoonful straight from the container.

POTATO SALAD

The Del prep kitchen's exact recipe was mixed by hand with a glove up to the elbow. Go for it!

Happily, here's the home kitchen-size recipe.

8 cups potatoes, peeled, cooked and cooled, cubed (about 3-4 pounds potatoes)

½ cup chopped sweet onion

½ cup chopped radishes

⅓ cup chopped pimentos or sweet peppers

YIELD: 4-6 SERVINGS

The bakery and deli were certified as kosher for a twenty-four-hour period in August 1974 so the Berenbergs could bring the famous potato salad along with other goodies to Camp Tikvah in Aitkin, Minnesota, for visitor's day. Guilt was obviously the motivating factor, as it was Tess and Morrie's oldest granddaughter's first time at overnight camp. Just sayin'.

8 hard-cooked eggs, peeled and coarsely chopped

1 teaspoon salt

1 tablespoon white pepper

1½ cups Miracle Whip

Combine all ingredients and gently toss. Refrigerate.

BIG BATCH PICKLED BEETS

18 #10 bulk units beets

15 sliced onions

2 cans beet juice

2 cans vinegar

2 cans sugar

1 cup pickling spices

Divide beets and onions among 3 (4-gallon) containers. Boil beet juice, vinegar, sugar, and pickling spices for 15 minutes. Strain liquid over beets and onions. Cover and chill.

TESS ALWAYS SAID,
"I MAKE ENOUGH TO FEED
AN ARMY."

"Big batch" is in the title because this was how we made and stored the beets that filled the silver bowls on each table.
In this original recipe, a can equals a gallon.

BREAKFAST
LUNCHEON
DINNER AND
LATE EVENING
SERVICE

COLESLAW *Craving*

Jane Dusek shares this memory—and a plea.

I HAD BEEN A HAPPY CUSTOMER of Lincoln Del for decades. Especially while I lived in Bloomington . . . anytime I had a bad migraine, I would stop by the Bloomington restaurant for a pint (or two) of chicken matzo ball soup, and it would fix me right up.

When word came in 2000 that the Del was closing its doors for good, I was heartbroken. Along with their soup, their grilled pastrami-and-pepper-jack-on-pumpernickel was another favorite classic. And then . . . there was the coleslaw. The *best* I'd ever had in my life. What was I going to do without it???

The only thing I could do was what I did the day the Del closed. I got to the St. Louis Park location, and I was the very *last* person in the door before the man in the white apron said behind me, "Okay, that's it. We are locking the doors. No one else comes in." I looked over to my right and saw the dining room full of customers. It was hard to imagine what they were thinking/feeling, enjoying their Last Del Meal.

But I turned to my left into the deli, and made a beeline for the deli counter. I parked myself in front of the big white plastic bucket of coleslaw that sat tantalizingly close, just on the other side of the glass.

A young man stepped up behind the counter across from me and asked, "May I help you?"

"I'll take the coleslaw," I said, my eyes never leaving my prize.

"How much would you like?" he queried.

Without hesitation I replied, "All of it."

He chuckled a bit at my response, "There's more than a little there."

I smiled. "I hope it's enough."

He packaged it in a couple smaller-sized buckets, I paid, and I was on my way.

The coleslaw lasted about three days, during which I tried my level best to figure out its recipe . . . to no avail.

The Taste and Food and Dining editors and research staff must be having a chuckle . . . or a grimace . . . right about now, as they may recognize my name. I have been calling both the Minneapolis and St. Paul papers *for years* asking, "Can you find/Can you *get* the Lincoln Del coleslaw recipe?"

So FINALLY . . . Here's My Chance!

PLEASE, OH PLEASE . . . Please include the Lincoln Del Coleslaw recipe! *L*

CELERY SEED COLESLAW

YIELD: 16 SERVINGS
We hope it lives up to the hype.

4 cups Miracle Whip

4 cups mayonaise

7 cups sugar

3 cups white vinegar

¾ teaspoon salt

¾ teaspoon pepper

¾ teaspoon dry mustard

1 large onion, chopped fine

½–1 cup celery seed

20 cups shredded cabbage (about 6–8 large heads)

Combine all ingredients except cabbage, mixing well. Fold in cabbage. Refrigerate.

LINCOLN DEL KOSHER DILLS

YIELD: 12 QUARTS

about 16 pounds pickling cucumbers

2 cloves garlic per jar

2 small chile peppers per jar

sprig of fresh dill per jar

pickling spices, optional

plain or kosher salt (not iodized)

cold water (not softened)

Thoroughly rinse cucumbers. Drain. Tip a quart canning jar. Pack larger cucumbers on bottom and smaller ones on top. Add garlic, chile peppers, dill, and pickling spices (if using) to each jar. Add 1 tablespoon salt to each jar, then fill with water. Loosely close self-sealing jar lids. Place jars on newspapers to soak up any leakage. (Most jars will leak somewhat. This isn't a problem. No need to re-tighten lids or use the upside-down treatment.) Let stand for 7 days. Tighten lids and place jars in cool place or refrigerator for storing. Best if eaten within 1 year.

THE PICKLE *Maven*

PICKLES ARE THE VERY HEART AND SOUL of all true deli operations. The pickles may be served whole, quartered, in slices, or sometimes as midgets. But not just any pickle: the pickle must be a garlic half-dill pickle, always kosher style, made with a saltwater brine, garlic, hot peppers, and dill. Notice: no preservatives, other than salt. And, never, never, never made with vinegar.

In the early days, the Lincoln Dels served each table complimentary "relish trays" of kosher dill pickles and pickled beets. This practice was copied from the famous delicatessen operations of Miami Beach, the Rascal House and Pumpernicks. Though very popular, the silver bowls of pickles and beets had to be removed from the tables in the early 1970s because the St. Louis Park Health Department prohibited them. By that time, the Dels were using more than two hundred gallons of pickles per day.

In the 1990s, Abe "Abie" Schwartz and Jake Garber, both close friends of Morrie Berenberg, encouraged the Del to produce a higher quality half-dill pickle than could be obtained on the commercial market. Abie was a master pickler—not only of kosher dills, but of green tomatoes, watermelon, carrots, and beans, and also of vishnick, a homebrew of bing cherries immersed in vodka. Danny Berenberg recruited Abie to partner with his son, Jake Berenberg, to produce high-quality kosher half-dills for retail sale. At the time, Abie was approaching ninety years of age and Jake was approaching eighteen. The union of two very independent thinkers, and the vast distance between their ages and backgrounds, made

Abie Schwartz, the "Pickle Maven"

their collaboration highly unlikely, but somehow the pairing worked, and the Del began producing hundreds of cases of kosher half-dills that became the rage of the local market, including at SuperValu and a number of other grocery chains in the Twin Cities. Orders began to pour in from across the country.

Both the pickles and the partnership were covered extensively by the press. The pickles proved so popular that it looked like an independent company might be formed. In fact, the Del had to negotiate contracts in California and Mexico to assure supply of cucumbers through the cold months.

The operation's demise came after Jake and Abe cornered the dill market in Minnesota. While many local suppliers grew cucumbers, the Del was unable to maintain a consistent stash of fresh dill. Eventually, Danny called upon the M. A. Gedney pickle company in Chaska, Minnesota, to share some of their dill reserves, which they generously did, until their own supply was jeopardized. The Del was forced to suspend manufacturing.

By then, Abie's pickles had become the standard on which all other kosher half-dill pickles were judged: no compromises. £

Sandwiches and Main Dishes

GRILLED REUBEN AND GRILLED RACHEL

REUBEN

4 tablespoons (½ stick) butter, softened

2 slices Pumpernickel (page 146) or Rye Bread (page 144), toasted

¼ pound sliced corned beef, not too lean

¼ cup sauerkraut

2 tablespoons mayonnaise

2 slices Swiss cheese

YIELD: 1 SANDWICH

Many who miss their regular nosh dates at the Del crave these very sandwiches, always served hot.

Spread butter on both sides of the toasted bread. Warm the corned beef by wrapping it in foil and heating in a 300-degree oven for 5 minutes. Warm the sauerkraut by placing it in the microwave for 1 minute. Preheat a griddle or skillet. Assemble the sandwich on the hot surface: 1 slice toast, spread with mayo, then stacked with 1 slice cheese, corned beef, sauerkraut, remaining slice cheese, and last slice of bread, spread with mayo. Top with a heavy press and grill for 2 minutes on each side to melt cheese. Slice in half and serve with one Kosher Dill Pickle (page 91) and Celery Seed Coleslaw (page 91).

RACHEL

4 tablespoons butter, softened

2 slices Pumpernickel (page 146) or Rye Bread (page 144), toasted

¼ pound sliced fresh turkey

¼ pound sliced corned beef, not too lean

2 tablespoons Thousand Island Dressing (page 86)

2 slices Swiss cheese ⟹

93

Butter both sides of the toasted bread. Warm the turkey and corned beef by wrapping each in foil and heating in a 300-degree oven for 5 minutes. Preheat a griddle or skillet. Assemble the sandwich on the hot surface: 1 slice toast spread with Thousand Island Dressing, 1 slice cheese, turkey and corned beef, remaining slice cheese, and last slice of bread, spread with Thousand Island Dressing. Top with a heavy press and grill for 2 minutes on each side to melt the cheese. Slice in half and serve with one Kosher Dill Pickle (page 91) and Celery Seed Coleslaw (page 91).

DELWICH

1 (6-ounce) ground beef patty
onion, chopped
sweet pepper (pimento), chopped
butter, softened
2 slices Pumpernickel Bread (page 146)
2 slices American cheese

YIELD: 1 SANDWICH
The name for this sandwich was coined as a combination of "deli" and "sandwich." The Delwich remained a big hit long after the Dels closed.

On a hot griddle or in a preheated skillet, grill ground beef patty to medium. Grill onions and sweet peppers. Butter pumpernickel slices and grill both sides, adding a slice of cheese to each. When the cheese melts, place beef patty on top and cover with grilled onion and sweet peppers. Cover with second cheese-and-bread slice, and serve with french fries and a pickle slice.

Other favorite sandwiches,
ingredients lists included

THE Lincoln DELUXE SANDWICHES

At the price we have to charge to serve LOX, we suggest you make a different choice from our menu.

GRILLED REUBEN
Corned Beef, Swiss Cheese, Sauerkraut, Mayonnaise on Fresh Pumpernickel with Potato Chips
4.25

ROMANIAN REUBEN
Grilled
Romanian Pastrami, Swiss Cheese, Kraut and Sour Cream on Rye Bread, Chips
4.25

DEL-WICH
Ground Beef and Melted Cheese, Diced Onion, Diced Sweet Peppers on Grilled Fresh Pumpernickel Served with French Fries
4.25

GRILLED RACHAEL
Swiss Cheese, Turkey, Corned Beef 1000 Island Dressing on Choice of Bread Potato Chips
4.25

FRENCH DIP
CORNED BEEF
ROAST BEEF
on Large French Roll Pitcher of Natural Gravy with French Fries
4.25

CANARY
Ground Beef on Sesame Bun Lettuce, Tomato and Onion French Fries
3.65

POOR BOY
Corned Beef on French Roll French Fries
4.25

DENVER
Corned Beef, Green Peppers, Eggs and Onions on a Sesame Bun with French Fries
4.25
With Melted Cheese **4.45**

HOGIE
Corned Beef, Pastrami, Salami and Bologna Cheese, Tomatoes, Lettuce and Onion on French Bread
5.95

MINNESOTA TWINS
Two Char-Broiled Miniature Hamburgers on Oven-Fresh French Rolls French Fries
3.60

VULTURE
Ground Beef on Large French Roll, Raw Onion, French Fries and Cole Slaw
4.75

LINCOLN TWINS
Two Over-stuffed Corned Beef Sandwiches on Our Own Oven-Fresh French Rolls Served with Potato Knish
4.25

TRIPLE TOOTSIE
Three Separate Tasty Sandwiches on Delicious French Rolls, Chopped Chicken Liver, Corned Beef, Pastrami and French Fries
4.95

PUMP — TWINS
Two Over-stuffed Corned Beef on Pumpernickel Rolls French Fries or Cole Slaw
4.25

LINCOLN COMBINATION
Pastrami and Corned Beef on a Large Onion Roll French Fries
4.25

BAGEL-MELT
Broiled Hamburger, Hot American Cheese, Bacon, Lettuce and Tomato Served Open Face on Bagel and Fries
4.25

BAR-B-Q BEEF on FRENCH ROLL
Generous Serving with Lincoln's Special Bar-B-Q Sauce and French Fries
4.25

"THE PEPPER SANDWICH"
Pastrami with Hot Pepper Cheese on a Choice of Oven Fresh Bread Served with Cole Slaw
4.25

Sandwiches

FULL ¼ LB. CORNED BEEF	2.95		HAMBURGER, BROILED	2.35
CORNED BEEF — SWISS CHEESE	3.45		CHEESEBURGER, BROILED	2.60
FULL ¼ LB. PASTRAMI	2.95		HOT DOG, Broiled w/Relish & Chips	2.15
TONGUE	3.25		BROILED KNOCKWURST Served Open Face w/Chips	2.50
CHOPPED CHICKEN LIVER	2.55		BACON, LETTUCE and TOMATO	2.45
FULL ¼ LB. ROAST BEEF w/chips	3.55		PEANUT BUTTER	1.35
FRESH ROASTED TURKEY (All White) with Lettuce and Mayonnaise	3.55		PEANUT BUTTER and BACON	2.55
			SALAMI or BOLOGNA and EGG	2.95
HARD SALAMI	3.15		FRIED EGG 1.70 w/Chips with Bacon	2.95
SOFT SALAMI	2.55		GRILLED CHEESE	1.70
BOLOGNA	2.55		GRILLED CHEESE, BACON & TOMATO w/Chips	3.15
BAKED HAM	3.50		LOX, CREAM CHEESE & ONION, Served Open Face on Bagel, 3 oz.	4.85
ALBACORE TUNA SALAD	3.00			
SALMON SALAD	3.15			
CHICKEN SALAD	2.95			
EGG SALAD	2.15			

25¢ Extra for Bagel or Kaiser Roll
30¢ Extra for Large Onion Roll or Large French Roll
25¢ Extra for Grilling

NO CREDIT CARDS ACCEPTED

LINCOLN DEL (VIENNA BEEF) CHICAGO-STYLE HOT DOGS

Follow the instructions for that yummy "snap" when you bite into this dog.

Vienna Beef Frankfurters
Chicago-style poppy seed hot dog buns
yellow mustard
freshly chopped onion
tomato wedges
Vienna Sport Peppers
Vienna Chicago Style Relish
celery salt
kosher pickles

Warm frankfurters in water (do not boil) and finish on a grill. Warm buns in a steamer. Place frankfurter in bun with yellow mustard, freshly chopped onion, tomato wedge, 2 sport peppers, and green relish; sprinkle with celery salt. Top with ¼ slice kosher pickle. Wrap in waxed paper and serve.

FROM THE *Vienna Sausage* CO.

THE "CHICAGO STYLE" HOT DOG history began with street cart hot dog venders during the hard times of the Great Depression. Money was scarce, but business was booming for these entrepreneurs who offered a delicious hot meal on a bun for only a nickel. The famous Chicago Style Hot Dog was born!

They'd start with a Vienna Beef hot dog, nestle it in a steamed poppy seed bun, and cover it with a wonderful combination of toppings: yellow mustard, bright green relish, fresh chopped onions, juicy red tomato wedges, a kosher-style pickle spear, a couple of spicy sport peppers and finally, a dash of celery salt.

This unique hot dog creation was a "salad on top" and its memorable interplay of hot and cold, crisp and soft, sharp and smooth, became America's original fast food and a true Chicago institution. *L*

HOT DOG *Hubbub*

DANNY BERENBERG TELLS A STORY about Dr. Larry Singher, a children's cancer specialist at Children's Hospital in Minneapolis.

Larry was my children's pediatrician and a very close friend for many years, so when he asked me to give his daughter, Tracy, a summer job, I, of course, accommodated. I summoned Tracy to the Del and asked her what she would be interested in doing for the summer. She said she wanted something outside, no weekends, no long hours, no limitation on visits from friends during work, no overtime, no uniform, liberal clothing allowance—[basically something] where she could set her own hours and would not be stressed by the demands of the job. Her job criteria suggested to me that she had executive aspirations. I offered an executive position that would seem to meet her requirements. I proposed that the Lincoln Del would be pleased to hire her as the Hot Dog Lady. This job consisted of selling hot dogs from a cart . . . over the lunch hour at Lincoln Del South. She could stay as long as she wanted each day. No weekends. She would be outdoors in the sun for the summer. She could wear whatever she liked. She accepted the position reluctantly.

First, I had to get a hot dog cart. I contacted Vienna Sausage Company in Chicago and asked how I might acquire a cart for Tracy. They said, "Come to Chicago," not wanting to discuss my request on the telephone. I traveled to Chicago only to be informed that the hot dog carts did not belong to them, but were the sole property of a colorful fellow on the local business scene. His name was Mr. Vito *something*, of course. I got his number from the sausage company and made an appointment.

I visited with Mr. Vito at a local pizza/spaghetti joint on the South Side to make my request. There, I was "welcomed" by several of Mr. Vito's associates and the boss himself. I explained that I had a deli in Minneapolis and I needed a hot dog cart to accommodate the summer employment of Dr. Larry Singher's daughter. I further explained that Dr. Singher was a pediatric oncologist who spends his life trying to save little kids with advanced cancer. Mr. Vito was moved, but only to a degree. He said that he couldn't allow any competition to spring up in Chicago "willy nilly," so if I took the hot dog cart, I would have to give my assurance that the cart would never return to Chicago under pain of broken limbs or possibly even death. I could see the reasonableness of his position instantly. I agreed. It seemed expeditious. Also, a fair price to pay was asked—the price was zero—only . . . that if his kid got cancer, Dr. Singher would take care of that, too. I didn't consult the doctor, not thinking it wise to do. I agreed. Mr. Vito ordered one of his associates (Mr. Vincenzo) to put the cart on one of their trucks to Minneapolis.

The cart arrived the very next day, and Tracy opened shop soon thereafter in her new position as executive director of street cart hot dog sales. Though sometimes Tracy would not show up for work (no complaints from me because of my liberal hour guarantee), when she was there the hot dog cart became a big hit. Virtually every day when she did come to work, there would be lines of cabs, trucks, and cars lined up in the drive in front of Lincoln Del South to purchase their hot dogs from Tracy and her cart. I suspect this popularity had something to do with the fact that she usually wore beach attire and the hot dogs sold for only $1.25 complete with bun and condiments. This was long before marketing through street vendors became popular, though I remember seeing some bikini-clad hot dog cart vendors in Fort Lauderdale the very next year.

This went on for nearly all summer. The popular phrase was "Meet me at the Del for a hot dog!" We sold tons of hot dogs. Caused daily traffic jams. And it all came to an end in August, when my father realized Tracy was selling the hot dogs at about half of our cost. I received orders to immediately shut down the hot dog cart operation and ship the cart back to Chicago. I invited Tracy for an executive lunch planning meeting. I did not want to let her know the predicament I was in with my father, so I simply asked her what her plans were for the rest of the summer. She immediately informed me that she had enough of the hot dog world; being the executive in charge of hot dog cart sales had become onerous. Her girl-friends were teasing her. The heat of the summer was becoming oppressive, and she really wanted to spend more time with her friends at the country club pool. Was I interested in a generous severance? Of course I was. The problem solved itself, save the order to return the hot dog cart to Chicago. I thought of contacting Mr. Vito about a return, and immediately thought better of it. In the end, I hid the cart in my garage until long after the death of my father.

The story might have ended there, but for Tracy being the delightful gal she was. She came to me years later to make an admission about something that had been troubling her ever since her hot dog cart summer. Now a grown and beauti-ful woman, both her father and mother having passed, she needed to tell me that she never learned how to make change, so for the entire summer of the hot dog cart, she simply took the money she was given by the hot dog buyers, and made no change. She was almost in tears when she made this admission to me, though Tracy always had a bit of the devil in her eyes. I told her it was okay. Now she really collapsed into tears. She said, "I cheated you after all you did for me that summer. . . . I cheated you—after your long friendship with my mother and father. . . . I cheated you after you saw my father through his cancer treatment, often tak-ing him back and forth to the hospital." I said, "Tracy—I always knew you couldn't make change!"

Now, Tracy is gone too. . . . All that is left is my wonderful memories of that beautiful summer. Hot dogs for a $1.25 or "something." Tracy in her swimsuits. The hot dog cart, never to be returned to Chicago under pain of mayhem. I loved all these people. Even Mr. Vito. Most of all Tracy. 𝓛

SWEET AND SOUR MEATBALLS

SAUCE

1 cup boiling water

⅔ cup packed brown sugar

⅔ cup granulated sugar

½ cup ketchup

juice of 2 lemons

1 (8-ounce) can tomato paste

MEATBALLS

2 pounds ground beef

2 teaspoons salt

3 teaspoons onion powder

½ teaspoon garlic salt

½ cup bread crumbs or matzo meal

½ cup chili sauce

1 large egg

YIELD: 12 SERVINGS

A big thank-you to Dr. Gabe Tarshish, who tested this recipe in his home kitchen in Louisville, Kentucky, on a rare afternoon when he wasn't working in pediatrics at the hospital or catching up on his beauty sleep.

In a pan large enough to hold the sauce and meatballs, whisk together boiling water, sugars, ketchup, and lemon juice until sugars are dissolved. Bring sauce to a slow boil, then reduce heat to simmer for 10 minutes. Stir in tomato paste.

Preheat oven to 325 degrees. Mix together meatball ingredients and form into golf ball-size portions. In a nonstick skillet set over medium heat, work in batches to lightly brown meatballs on all sides. Transfer meatballs to rimmed baking sheet and bake 30 minutes. Add meatballs to the simmering sauce and cook for about 10 minutes.

SPAGHETTI AND MEATBALLS

YIELD: 6-8 SERVINGS
A favorite of kids and adults alike.

SAUCE

2½ pounds ground beef

4 cups (two 16-ounce cans) crushed tomatoes

2 cups ketchup

3 cups tomato puree

½ cup sugar

¾ teaspoon dried rosemary

¾ teaspoon dried basil

¾ teaspoon dried thyme

1–2 cloves garlic, crushed

¼ cup beef soup base

¼ cup Worcestershire sauce

¼ cup canola oil

MEATBALLS

2½ pounds ground beef

½ teaspoon salt

¾ teaspoon pepper

¾ teaspoon garlic powder

½ cup bread crumbs

1 large egg

¼ cup finely chopped onion

1 pound pasta, cooked

For sauce, in a large pot or Dutch oven, brown beef; drain fat. Add remaining sauce ingredients and bring to boiling. Reduce heat to simmer and cook, covered, for 45 minutes, stirring frequently. Add water to reach desired consistency.

Meanwhile, make meatballs. In a large bowl, combine meatball ingredients, mixing well. Form into large meatballs. Cook in a lightly oiled pan until browned on all sides. Add to simmering sauce and cook over medium heat for 20 minutes. Serve sauce over pasta.

"RECIPES FROM THE *Lincoln Del*"

BY RICK NELSON, *STAR TRIBUNE*, APRIL 22, 2015

IN 2000, WITHIN WEEKS of the end of the Lincoln Del—the restaurant's roots reached back to 1935—a number of diners contacted the *Star Tribune*'s Restaurant Requests column (a forum for tracking down recipes to favorite restaurant dishes), asking if the Del would share its cabbage borscht recipe.

Taste staffer Diane Osby tracked down a recipe that had been published in the February 2000 issue of *Midwest Living* magazine, and the recipe reappeared in the June 8, 2000 edition of Taste.

Turns out, there was a hitch. A few weeks later, Lincoln Del owner Danny Berenberg revealed the following to *Star Tribune* gossip columnist CJ:

"I was at my mother's house for dinner the other night and [she] said, 'You know that article in the *Star Tribune* about the borscht? That isn't the right borscht recipe.' Berenberg said he tried to explain. 'Yeah, but that is an adaptation done by *Midwest Living* [magazine].' She said, 'But the ingredients aren't right.' This constant argument about are you really honest [with the] recipe, I think the way we are going to solve that is: In the cookbook we are going to give both—an adaption you can make at home and the bulk one— it makes 42 gallons."

In short, take this recipe with a grain of sour salt. *L*

CABBAGE BORSCHT

2 tablespoons butter, vegetable oil, clarified
    butter, or, even better, schmaltz (see note)
½ pound beef shank bones with marrow
1 pound rib eye steak or brisket, not too lean
5 cups unsalted beef stock or broth
2 medium tomatoes, chopped
⅔ cup ketchup

YIELD: 6 SERVINGS
This soup boasts a slightly sweet, incredibly addictive flavor made with love over generations. And, when meat was a rare commodity, the vegetarian version was equally delicious.

¼ cup sugar or 1 packet Truvia or other sweetener, to taste

1 teaspoon sour salt or citric acid (see note)

½ teaspoon pepper

2 pounds red cabbage, sliced in bite-size pieces

Warm butter or oil in 4-quart Dutch oven or stock pot over high heat. Brown shank bones and steak or brisket. Carefully add beef stock, tomatoes, ketchup, sweetener, sour salt, and pepper to pot; stir. Bring to boiling; reduce heat. Cover and simmer for 1 hour.

Remove meat from pot; cool slightly. Discard skin and fat. Cut meat into bite-size pieces. Return meat and any bones still filled with marrow to the pot. Stir in the cabbage, bring the mixture to a boil, then reduce heat. Cover and simmer for 10 minutes or until cabbage is crisp-tender.

NOTES: Clarified butter or schmaltz is preferable because each tolerates high temperatures without burning. Find them at the grocery store.

Sour salt is white powder extracted from the juice of citrus and other acidic fruits—lemons, limes, pineapples, etc. Find it with canning ingredients in the supermarket or order online. Also known as citric acid, it has a strong, tart taste and is used to flavor foods and beverages. Great for sweet and sour dishes, it is essential to our borscht recipe.

NOODLE KUGEL

1 (8-ounce) package cream cheese, softened
8 tablespoons (1 stick) butter, softened
½ cup sugar
½ cup milk, warmed
4 large eggs
1 cup raisins softened in warm water and
    drained, optional
1 (12-ounce) bag egg noodles cooked al dente

YIELD: 12 SERVINGS
This amazing recipe originated in the Berenberg family kitchen. Like most hungry kugel fans, we too fought over the crispy corner pieces.

Preheat oven to 350 degrees. Grease a 9x13-inch glass pan. In bowl of stand mixer, combine cream cheese and butter and beat on medium speed until fluffy. Add sugar, beat for 1 minute, then add milk, beating until cooled. Beat each egg separately and add one at a time to the mixture, blending at low speed. Stir in raisins (if using). Gently fold in the cooked noodles by hand. Pour mixture into prepared pan. Bake for 1½ to 2 hours, until noodles are a bit crispy on top.

RICE PUDDING

6 large eggs
4 cups milk or heavy cream
2 cups cooked rice
4 tablespoons (½ stick) butter, softened
1 cup white or brown sugar
1 cup raisins
¼ teaspoon cinnamon
¼ teaspoon nutmeg
¼ teaspoon salt
1 teaspoon vanilla

YIELD: 8 SERVINGS
An old-time favorite, enhanced with raisins if you dare. Great warm or cold.

Preheat oven to 325 degrees. Grease a 9-inch square or round glass baking dish. In a large bowl, stir together all ingredients, then transfer to prepared pan. Bake for approximately 60 minutes.

CHEESE BLINTZES AND CHEESE BAGELACH

FILLING

2 cups dry or farmer cheese, or substitute dry
   cottage cheese

2 cups baker's cheese (see note page 106)

1½ cups (3 sticks) butter, softened

½ cup sugar

4 large eggs

1¼ teaspoons salt

FOR BLINTZES

4 large eggs

1 cup milk

1 cup water

2 cups flour

pinch salt

FOR BAGELACH

16 tablespoons (2 sticks) cold butter, chopped

1 cup all-purpose flour

zest of ½ lemon

1 teaspoon salt

8 ounces cream cheese, chilled

¼ cup sour cream

1–2 large eggs

YIELD: 24 BLINTZES OR 6-8 BAGELACH

Two options as vessels for the cheese filling, each with their own dough: lighter and flaky in a figure eight shape for bagelach, a rectangle in form for blintzes. Complement with jam and sour cream.

Preheat oven to 350 degrees. Prepare baking sheets with nonstick spray or parchment paper. Combine filling ingredients, mixing well. Set aside.

For blintzes, whisk together eggs, milk, and water. Stir in flour and salt and mix well by hand. On a well-floured work surface, roll dough into an 8x12–inch rectangle. Cut into 24 squares. Add 2 tablespoons of filling to each square and roll over once, "burrito style," then tuck in sides and fold again, pressing to seal. Set on prepared baking sheet, and bake for 15 minutes, until golden. ⟹

For bagelach, combine butter, flour, and lemon zest in a large bowl, rubbing together with fingertips until mixture resembles wet sand. Add salt, cream cheese, and sour cream, using hands to work into the flour until mixture is crumbly and only pea-size chunks of cream cheese remain. Press dough into a thick disk, wrap tightly in plastic wrap, and refrigerate for at least 20 minutes or overnight.

Beat egg(s) in a small bowl. On a well-floured work surface, roll chilled dough into an 8x16-inch rectangle. Trim any irregular edges. Spread some filling along the short edge of the dough and brush a little egg wash next to the filling. Slice pastry at the edge of the egg wash, then gently roll pastry around the filling, pressing into egg-wash section to seal in a cylinder shape. Bend bagelach into a figure eight and set on prepared baking sheet. Repeat with remaining pastry and filling to make 6 to 8 bagelach. Brush bagelach with additional egg wash and bake for 30 to 40 minutes, until golden brown. Serve warm, topped with jam and sour cream.

NOTE: Baker's cheese is a fresh, soft cheese not unlike cottage cheese. Made with skim milk, it has more moisture and is softer than cottage cheese. Farmer cheese is a close cousin. In England, it's called Colwick or cottager's cheese. Substituting ricotta will yield a softer consistency.

Pies

PIE CRUST

2½ cups flour

1 teaspoon salt

1 cup shortening or butter, chilled and cut into pieces

3 or more tablespoons cold water (see note)

YIELD: DOUGH FOR 9-INCH (2-CRUST) PIE

The original Del recipe used shortening rather than butter.

Combine flour and salt in a food processor and pulse gently, or combine in a mixer set on low speed. Add shortening or butter to the flour mixture and toss gently to coat, pulsing or mixing until the texture is the size of small peas. Gently blend in 3 tablespoons cold water, adding more water if the dough is dry. Try not to overwork the dough. As soon as the dough forms into a ball, dump onto a large sheet of waxed or parchment paper and pat into an oval shape. Cut in half and wrap each in waxed paper or plastic. Chill for at least 1 hour and up to 24 in the refrigerator before rolling out on a well-floured surface to use as directed.

To prebake: preheat oven to 350 degrees. Roll out half the dough into a 10-inch circle. Pat into a 9-inch pie pan. Line crust with parchment paper and fill with dried beans or pie weights. Bake until crust is lightly browned, about 15 to 20 minutes. Carefully lift and remove paper with pie weights, and let crust cool.

NOTE: For a flakier crust, in place of the water, Kit substitutes cold vanilla vodka for sweet pies and unflavored vodka for savory pies.

CHOCOLATE PIE

Wendi has received the most bribery attempts over this recipe. Offers of money and fame. Marriage and adoption proposals. Sad, pathetic pleadings from people around the world. All who love the Del's chocolate cream pie ask this most important question: frozen or thawed? Those who swear by the orgasmic first bite they chisel off a frozen slice of heaven can't imagine it eaten any other way. Some purists even discard the real whipped cream topping and the flaky crust to focus only on the chocolate.

YIELD: 1 (9-INCH) PIE
Nope: no extra forks. Few will share this flavor sensation.

2½ cups confectioner's sugar
⅔ cup unsweetened dark cocoa powder
⅓ cup shortening or butter
½ cup warm water (see note)
8 tablespoons (1 stick) butter, softened
1¾ cups granulated sugar
1 teaspoon vanilla
4 large pasteurized eggs
1 (9-inch) prebaked pie crust (see page 107)
Whipped Cream (page 125) for serving
shaved chocolate for serving

Prepare chocolate liquor by placing confectioner's sugar, cocoa, and shortening in a large bowl and blending on low speed until smooth. Slowly blend in warm water. Set aside to cool.

Place 8 tablespoons butter, granulated sugar, and vanilla in bowl of stand mixer and blend on low speed until smooth. Slowly add ½ cup of the cooled chocolate liquor and eggs. Scrape sides of the bowl and then mix on medium speed until fluffy. Pour filling into pie shell, cover with plastic wrap, and refrigerate or freeze for 24 hours before serving. Decorate with whipped cream and shaved chocolate.

NOTE: Kit prefers to use strong, dark coffee in place of the hot water. The extra chocolate liquor will keep in a sealed jar in the refrigerator for up to one month.

Chocolate Pie. Photo by Sam Stern

"LINCOLN DEL TIPS YIELD *Sweet New Treats*"

ANN BURCKHARDT'S ARTICLE, published in the *Minneapolis Star* on November 1, 1978, highlighted some Del secrets. The Del's professional pastry chef, Daniel Hemiadan, shared that the Del's top-selling pie was the chocolate cream pie and the top cake was the chocolate whipped cream cake, which remained the most popular until the Del closed in 2000. Hemiadan was critical in the process of calculating the recipes collected here from bulk size to home use. At the time of the article, he noted that many bakery items were not originally produced with home baking in mind. Ingredients such as chocolate liquor and 40 percent fat whipped cream could be found only at food service outlets open to the trade and not the general public. The 1978 article shared two recipes with readers, Chocolate Chip Cookies (page 129) and Egg Bagels (page 138), both "Lincoln Del Style." *L*

PECAN PIE

3 large eggs
⅔ cup sugar
⅓ cup butter, melted
1 cup dark corn syrup
2 cups pecan halves, divided
½ teaspoon salt
½ teaspoon vanilla
1 (9-inch) prebaked pie crust (see page 107)

YIELD: 1 (9-INCH) PIE
Countless family members have admitted to eating the whole pie in one sitting, armed with only a spoon and a glass of milk.

Preheat oven to 350 degrees. Mix together eggs, sugar, butter, corn syrup, 1 cup pecan halves, salt, and vanilla. Pour mixture into prebaked pie crust and sprinkle remaining 1 cup pecans on top. Bake for 1 hour, until golden brown.

LEMON MERINGUE PIE

3 cups cold water
¾ cup cornstarch, divided
4 tablespoons (½ stick) butter
1 tablespoon lemon zest
¾ cup lemon juice
1 cup sugar
¾ teaspoon salt
3 large egg yolks
1 (9-inch) prebaked pie crust (see page 107)
Meringue (recipe follows)

YIELD: 1 (9-INCH) PIE
Refreshingly tart. Offered in one-serving size and "regular" size.

Whisk together 1 cup cold water and ¼ cup cornstarch. In a medium saucepan, combine water and cornstarch slurry, remaining 2 cups water, remaining ½ cup cornstarch, butter, lemon zest and juice, sugar, and salt. Bring to a light boil, whisking constantly until sugar is dissolved and mixture is thick. Place ⅓ cup of the hot mixture in a small bowl, and stir in egg yolks until well combined. Slowly add the mixture back into the saucepan and continue to boil lightly, stirring well, until mixture thickens, about 5 minutes. Remove from heat and pour into prepared pie crust. Cover with plastic wrap and refrigerate until set, 3 hours or up to 1 day.

Preheat oven to 350 degrees. Prepare meringue. Pile meringue on pie, making sure it touches the crust all around. Bake until meringue begins to brown, 8 to 10 minutes.

MERINGUE

8 large egg whites

½ cup superfine sugar (see note page 124)

¼ teaspoon coarse salt

In a large bowl, combine egg whites, sugar, and salt. Use an electric mixer to beat on medium-high speed until stiff peaks form.

APPLE PIE

14 Braeburn apples (2–3 pounds), peeled, cored, and cut into ½-inch slices

1 cup lemon juice

1¼ cups granulated sugar, divided

½ cup packed brown sugar

1 teaspoon cinnamon

½ cup flour

pastry dough for double-crust 9-inch pie, bottom crust prebaked (page 107)

8 tablespoons (1 stick) butter

YIELD: 1 (9-INCH) PIE
In the Berenberg kitchen we piled the apples high and placed huge chunks of butter on the mound of deliciousness before setting the top crust. Then we waited impatiently for the gooey goodness to come out of the oven, to be complemented with a scoop of cinnamon ice cream.

Preheat oven to 350 degrees. Place apple slices in a large bowl and soak with lemon juice. In a separate large bowl, mix together 1 cup granulated sugar, brown sugar, and cinnamon. Drain apples and add them to the sugar mixture, tossing to thoroughly coat. Stir in flour, mixing well to coat   ⟹

the apples evenly. Pour the apple mixture into prebaked pie crust, mounding up to 3 inches above the pan. Cut 4 tablespoons butter into 6 pieces and distribute on top of the apples. Cover with unbaked pie crust, crimping the edges. Cut four 1-inch slits in top crust to ventilate. Melt remaining 4 tablespoons butter, stir in remaining ¼ cup granulated sugar, and brush on top of the pie. Bake for 45 minutes, until the crust is golden brown.

PUMPKIN PIE

YIELD: 1 (8-INCH) PIE
It's not just for Thanksgiving!

1 (9-inch) pastry crust

1 cup sugar

2 tablespoons tapioca starch

½ teaspoon cinnamon

½ teaspoon nutmeg

pinch ground ginger

½ teaspoon salt

1¾ cups pumpkin purée

1⅓ cups evaporated milk

1 cup half-and-half

2 large eggs

1 teaspoon vanilla

Preheat oven to 325 degrees. Line an 8-inch pie plate with pastry dough. In bowl of stand mixer, combine sugar, tapioca starch, cinnamon, nutmeg, ginger, and salt. Mix on low speed for 2 minutes, then gradually add pumpkin, evaporated milk, half-and-half, eggs, and vanilla, mixing well to combine. Pour mixture into pie shell and bake for approximately 45 minutes or until the pie filling is firm.

Cakes

BUTTER SPONGE CAKE

7 large eggs

1½ cups confectioner's sugar

½ teaspoon salt

1 teaspoon vanilla

1½ teaspoons baking powder

2¾ cups cake flour, sifted

2 cups (4 sticks) butter, melted and cooled

YIELD: 2 (8-INCH) CAKE LAYERS

For Frogs (page 128), Strawberry Shortcake (page 117), and Lemon Coconut Layer Cake (page 118).

Preheat oven to 400 degrees. Grease 2 (8-inch) round or square springform cake pans. In bowl of stand mixer, combine eggs, confectioner's sugar, and salt and beat on medium speed until light yellow. Beat in vanilla and baking powder. Fold in the flour by hand. Fold in the cooled melted butter. Pour batter into prepared pans. Bake for 40 minutes or until a wooden pick inserted in the middle comes out clean.

WHITE CAKE

3½ cups cake flour

1¾ cups sugar

½ cup powdered milk

3½ tablespoons cornstarch

1 tablespoon baking powder

1 teaspoon salt

dash cream of tartar

¾ cup shortening

2½ tablespoons corn syrup

1 tablespoon vanilla

1 large egg plus 6 large egg whites   ⟹

YIELD: 2 (8-INCH) CAKE LAYERS

Tess always called it "Lady Baltimore" cake.

Preheat oven to 350 degrees. Grease and flour 2 (8-inch) cake pans. In bowl of stand mixer, combine flour, sugar, powdered milk, cornstarch, baking powder, salt, cream of tartar, shortening, corn syrup, vanilla, whole egg, and 2/3 cup water. Blend at medium speed for 3 minutes. In a separate bowl, beat egg whites on medium speed until fluffy. Gently fold egg whites into batter. Pour batter into prepared pans. Bake for 20 to 35 minutes, until wooden pick inserted in the middle comes out clean.

CHOCOLATE CAKE

YIELD: 4 (8-INCH) CAKE LAYERS
Be careful not to overbake.

4 large eggs plus 2 large egg whites

3 cups cake flour

¾ cup unsweetened cocoa powder

4½ tablespoons powdered milk

3½ tablespoons cornstarch

1½ tablespoons baking powder

1½ tablespoons baking soda

1½ teaspoons salt

2 cups sugar

¾ cup shortening or butter, softened

3½ tablespoons dark corn syrup

1½ teaspoons vanilla

Preheat oven to 375 degrees. Grease and flour 4 (8-inch) cake pans. In a medium bowl, combine whole eggs, egg whites, and ⅓ cup water. Use a mixer to blend for 3 minutes; set aside. In a small bowl, whisk together flour, cocoa, powdered milk, cornstarch, baking powder, baking soda, and salt. In bowl of stand mixer, combine sugar and shortening. Mix at medium speed for 1 minute. Add ⅓ cup water, corn syrup, egg mixture, and vanilla and mix at medium speed for 3 minutes. Scrape the bowl, add flour mixture, and blend on medium speed for 2 minutes. Pour batter into prepared pans. Bake for 25 to 30 minutes, until wooden pick inserted in the middle comes out clean. Cool on a rack for 30 minutes before removing from pans.

FOR CHOCOLATE WHIPPED CREAM CAKE

Spread cooled layers of Chocolate Cake with fresh Whipped Cream (page 125), cover with more real whipped cream, and top with crumbled chocolate cake.

GERMAN CHOCOLATE CAKE

¾ cup semisweet chocolate chips

¾ cup water

1 tablespoon vanilla

1 teaspoon salt

3½ cups cake flour

2 teaspoons baking soda

2 cups sugar

12 tablespoons (1½ sticks) butter, softened

½ cup shortening

4 large eggs, separated

1½ cups buttermilk

German Chocolate Frosting (recipe follows)

YIELD: 1 (8-INCH) DOUBLE-LAYER CAKE

This recipe could also be made as bars in 2 eight-inch-square pans. Never enough gooey goodness here!

Preheat oven to 350 degrees. Grease and flour 2 (8-inch) cake pans. In a small saucepan over low heat, combine chocolate chips, water, vanilla, and salt. Melt chocolate, stirring to combine. Set aside to cool. Whisk together flour and baking soda. In bowl of stand mixer, combine sugar, butter, and shortening and blend on medium speed for 4 minutes. Gradually stir in cooled chocolate mixture, then add egg yolks and buttermilk, blending until well mixed. Stir in flour mixture. In a separate bowl, whip egg whites to stiff peaks. Gently fold the whipped egg whites into the cake batter. Pour batter into prepared pans and bake for 25 to 30 minutes, until a wooden pick inserted in the middle comes out clean. Let cakes cool, remove from pans, and cut each horizontally into 2 layers. Fill the layers and frost the outside of cake with German Chocolate Frosting. ⟹

GERMAN CHOCOLATE FROSTING

2½ cups evaporated milk

7 large egg yolks

2½ cups (5 sticks) butter, melted

2½ cups sugar

3 cups pecan pieces

3½ cups sweetened flaked coconut

In a saucepan set over medium heat, stir together evaporated milk, egg yolks, butter, and sugar. Cook, stirring, over medium heat for 15 minutes. Remove from heat and stir in pecans and coconut. Allow frosting to cool before frosting cake.

BOSTON CREAM PIE

1 cup shortening

1¾ cups cake flour

1 cup sugar

3 tablespoons plus ¾ teaspoon baking powder

1½ tablespoons powdered milk

2 teaspoons salt

6 large eggs

1 tablespoon vanilla

Custard Filling (recipe follows)

Chocolate Glaze (recipe follows)

YIELD: 1 (8-INCH) DOUBLE-LAYER CAKE
Be careful not to overbake.

Preheat oven to 350 degrees. Grease and flour 2 (8-inch) cake pans. In bowl of stand mixer, combine shortening, flour, sugar, baking powder, powdered milk, salt, and 1 cup water. Mix on medium speed for 6 minutes. In a separate bowl, stir together eggs, ⅓ cup water, and vanilla. With the mixer running on low speed, add egg mixture in two portions. Mix until smooth. Divide batter between prepared cake pans and bake for 15 to 20 minutes, until golden and a wooden pick inserted in the middle comes out clean. Set aside to cool. Prepare Custard Filling and allow to cool. Place one cake on a serving platter, spread with custard filling, and top with second cake layer. Spread warm Chocolate Glaze over top of cake, letting it drizzle down the sides.

CUSTARD FILLING
4 cups whole milk
1½ cups sugar
¼ teaspoon salt
4 tablespoons (½ stick) butter
4½ tablespoons cornstarch
1 egg yolk
2 tablespoons vanilla

In a large saucepan set over low to medium heat, stir together milk, sugar, salt, and butter. Bring to a boil, stirring constantly. In a medium bowl, stir together cornstarch, egg yolk, and vanilla, then stir in 1 cup of hot milk mixture. Add mixture to saucepan, stirring constantly for 3 to 5 minutes. Cool custard before filling cake.

CHOCOLATE GLAZE
1 cup chocolate chips
¼ cup (½ stick) butter
1½ tablespoons light corn syrup
½ teaspoon vanilla

In a double boiler over hot, but not boiling water, combine chocolate chips, butter, and corn syrup. Stir until chips are melted and mixture is smooth; remove from heat, then stir in vanilla.

STRAWBERRY SHORTCAKE

1½ cups water

1¾ cups sugar

3½ tablespoons cornstarch

2 tablespoons plus ¾ teaspoon corn syrup

¼ cup strawberry jam

3 layers Butter Sponge Cake (1½ recipes, page 113)

Whipped Cream (page 125)

fresh strawberries

YIELD: 1 (3-LAYER) CAKE
Morrie Berenberg's favorite, featured in a Star Tribune article celebrating the opening of the second Lincoln Del, on Highways 12 and 100 (see page 32).

In large saucepan, combine water, sugar, cornstarch, corn syrup, and jam. Set over medium-high heat and bring to boiling. Cook, stirring occasionally, until the glaze is clear and lightly colored. Top 1 cake layer with whipped cream and sliced strawberries; add another cake layer and top with whipped cream and sliced strawberries; repeat with final layer, topping with whole strawberries. Drizzle with glaze upon request.

LEMON COCONUT LAYER CAKE

YIELD: 1 (8-INCH) DOUBLE-LAYER CAKE
This cake, a favorite of Wendi's grandmother-in-law Charlotte Wolfson, was often hand-delivered to Philadelphia. It is still a source of delightful memories for Wendi's mother-in-law, Elaine Wolfson Rosenstein. Not only does the coconut-lemony goodness look amazing, the cake works well cut in small squares as a "high tea" version.

zest of 8 Meyer lemons

3 cups sugar

16 tablespoons (2 sticks) unsalted butter, softened

8 large eggs

1 cup lemon juice (8–9 Meyer lemons)

¼ teaspoon kosher salt

1 cup sweetened flaked coconut, plus more for topping

White Cake (page 113) or Butter Sponge Cake (page 113)

To bowl of food processor fitted with a steel blade add zest and sugar and pulse to combine. In bowl of stand mixer, blend butter until creamy, then mix in sugar-lemon mixture. Add eggs, one at a time, blending well, and then mix in lemon juice and salt. Pour into a 2-quart saucepan and cook over low heat until mixture reaches 170 degrees and thickens, about 10 minutes, stirring constantly. Remove from heat and allow to cool.

Stir coconut into lemon curd. Spread filling between layers of cooled White Cake or Butter Sponge Cake as well as on top and sides. Sprinkle additional coconut on the top and sides of the cake. Don't forget the cherry on top!

RUM CAKE

4¾ cups water, divided
7½ cups sugar, divided
1⅓ cups corn syrup
1½ teaspoons rum flavoring
2¾ cups cake flour
2 tablespoons baking powder
1 tablespoon powdered milk
¾ teaspoon salt
1 cup shortening
½ teaspoon vanilla
6 large eggs
1–2 cups chopped nuts, optional

YIELD: 1 LARGE OR 6 MINI BUNDT CAKES

One of the Del's most requested recipes. Delight your adult friends with the addition of rum rather than rum flavoring. Best made using individual medium Bundt pans, but worth a bake in mini Bundts for pop-in-your-mouth treats.

Preheat oven to 350 degrees. Grease and flour a 6-inch Bundt pan or 6 mini Bundt pans. In a large stockpot, combine 4 cups water, 4½ cups sugar, and corn syrup. Bring to a boil, remove from heat, and stir in rum flavoring. Set aside to cool.

In bowl of stand mixer, combine flour, remaining 3 cups sugar, baking powder, powdered milk, salt, shortening, vanilla, and remaining ¾ cup water. Blend on low speed for 1 minute, then on medium speed for 5 minutes. Add eggs, scrape sides of bowl, and mix on medium speed for 5 minutes.

⟹

Sprinkle nuts (if using) into prepared Bundt pan(s), then pour in batter. Bake smaller pans for 20 minutes, large pan for 30 minutes or until golden brown.

Cool cake(s) on wire rack for 10 minutes. Remove cake(s) from pan. Slowly lower cake(s) into the syrup until covered, then remove and place on a parchment paper-lined rack to cool. Extra syrup can be stored in a sealed jar in the refrigerator.

CARROT CAKE

YIELD: 1 (8-INCH) DOUBLE-LAYER CAKE
With thick cream cheese frosting, this cake is extra decadent.

1½ cups canola oil

2 large eggs

2 teaspoons vanilla

1 (8-ounce) can crushed pineapple, drained

2¾ cups cake flour

2 cups sugar

2 teaspoons baking soda

3 teaspoons cinnamon

1 teaspoon nutmeg

¼ teaspoon cloves

½ teaspoon salt

2 cups sweetened flaked coconut

2 cups shredded carrots

1 cup chopped walnuts

1 cup golden raisins, soaked for 15 minutes in warm water, drained, pressed, and patted dry

Cream Cheese Frosting (page 124)

Preheat oven to 350 degrees. Grease 2 (8-inch) cake pans and line with waxed or parchment paper. In a large bowl, stir together oil, eggs, vanilla, and pineapple. In another large bowl, stir together flour, sugar, baking soda, cinnamon, nutmeg, cloves, salt, coconut, carrots, walnuts, and raisins. Add dry ingredients to wet, mixing well by hand. Divide batter into prepared pans. Bake for 20 minutes; reduce heat to 275 degrees and bake an additional 15 minutes, until wooden pick inserted in the middle comes out clean. Cool in pan. Fill the layers and frost the outside of the cake with Cream Cheese Frosting.

CHOCOLATE CHIP DATE NUT CAKE

1 cup chopped dates

1 teaspoon baking soda

1 cup hot water

1 cup sugar

16 tablespoons (2 sticks) butter, softened

2 eggs

1¾ cups flour

1 teaspoon unsweetened cocoa powder

1 teaspoon vanilla

1 cup (or more) chocolate chips

½ cup (or more) nuts

**YIELD:
1 (9X13-INCH) CAKE**

This recipe originated in Tess Berenberg's kitchen and rarely lasted an hour out of the oven. Many tongues were burned by hot chocolate chips. Baubie Tess included on her recipe card the note "(or more)" next to the amounts of chocolate chips and nuts because she knew we loved a densely filled cake. We also liked to bake it in a loaf pan for a change of pace.

Preheat oven to 350 degrees. Grease and flour a 9x13-inch baking pan. Stir together dates, baking soda, and hot water; set aside to cool. In bowl of stand mixer, combine sugar, butter, and eggs; blend on medium speed until fluffy. Add flour, cocoa, vanilla, chocolate chips, and nuts. Drain dates and add to the bowl. Mix well. Pour batter into prepared pan; top with extra chips and nuts as desired. Bake for 40 minutes, until a wooden pick inserted in the middle comes out clean. Cool in pan before turning out to serve.

THE Koop Cake

PART OF THE DEL'S MARKETING STRATEGY was to regularly introduce new products. One such product was a forty-pound, *six-layer* chocolate devil's food cake iced with chocolate fudge frosting. Public relations expert Dave Mona came up with a great campaign to introduce the cake through local TV stations and the *Minneapolis Star and Tribune*. But on the launch date, Surgeon General C. Everett Koop made national news by releasing a public warning that sugar and sweets were killing the American public.

Dave called Danny Berenberg in a state of agitation: "What should we do? Should we pull back on the PR blitz?" Danny said, "Hell, no! We'll just rename the cake; we'll call it the Koop Cake." Mona amended the releases, and, of course, the local media got in on the joke. Each slice of the cake at Lincoln Del restaurants was the equivalent in weight to an entire seven-inch chocolate devil's food cake.

The story might have ended there if General Koop hadn't come to St. Paul for a conference. The surgeon general called Danny and asked if the Del had actually named the monstrous cake after him, as the press claimed. Danny replied that, indeed, he had filched Koop's name. Danny and Dave both knew that due to Koop's status as a public figure there wasn't much he could do about it, unless they fraudulently claimed some health benefit. Koop took the abuse of his name in good spirits and asked to see the cake. Danny had the cake delivered to him at the St. Paul Radisson. The general asked the delivery driver whether he could sample the cake. He was told he was welcome to the whole cake, but if he wanted to eat it, he must pay for it. He paid. *L*

CHEESECAKE

6½ cups crushed graham crackers

1¾ cups sugar, divided

1⅕ cups (2 sticks plus 3 tablespoons) butter, melted, plus 4 tablespoons (½ stick), softened

1 tablespoon cinnamon

3 (8-ounce) packages cream cheese, softened

1½ tablespoons cornstarch

2⅓ cups sour cream

1 cup heavy cream

2½ tablespoons water

4 large eggs

YIELD: 1 (8-INCH) CHEESECAKE

At home, Tess Berenberg made a thick layer of graham cracker crust on the bottom and sides of the cheesecake.

Preheat oven to 325 degrees. Grease bottom of an 8-inch springform pan. Stir together graham cracker crumbs, ¾ cup sugar, melted butter, and cinnamon until well mixed. Press into bottom and up sides of pan. Bake for 15 minutes; cool. Place pan inside another baking pan and fill outside pan with 1 inch water.

In bowl of stand mixer, combine cream cheese, softened butter, remaining 1 cup sugar, and cornstarch. Mix on low speed until no lumps remain. Gradually add sour cream, heavy cream, water, and eggs, mixing on low speed until smooth. Pour mixture into prepared pan. Bake for 40 to 45 minutes, until top is firm and center does not jiggle when gently shaken.

BUTTERCREAM FROSTING

YIELD: 6 CUPS, ENOUGH FOR 3 CAKES

9 cups superfine or confectioner's sugar
  (see note)
2½ cups shortening
12 tablespoons (1½ sticks) butter, softened
1 teaspoon salt
1 teaspoon vanilla

In bowl of stand mixer, combine ingredients and blend on low speed until mixed. Increase speed to medium and blend for 6 minutes, scraping sides of bowl as needed. Blend on medium speed for another 4 minutes, adding teaspoon amounts of water until the desired consistency is reached.

CREAM CHEESE FROSTING

YIELD: 2 CUPS, ENOUGH FOR 1 CAKE

8 tablespoons (1 stick) butter, softened
1 (8-ounce) package cream cheese, softened
3 cups superfine or confectioner's sugar, divided
1 teaspoon vanilla
1 teaspoon orange juice

In bowl of stand mixer, combine butter, cream cheese, and 1 cup confectioner's sugar. Blend on medium speed until mixed. Add vanilla and orange juice and blend on high for 1 minute. Add remaining 2 cups confectioner's sugar and mix well.

NOTE: To make 9 cups superfine sugar, blend 9⅓ cups granulated sugar in a food processor for 30 to 60 seconds.

With frosting, it's always good to double the recipe—to allow generous amounts of frosting between layers. Yum!

WHIPPED CREAM

1½ teaspoons unflavored gelatin powder or 2 packets
  whipped cream stabilizer (see note)
1½ tablespoons cold water
1½ cups heavy cream, chilled
5 tablespoons confectioner's sugar
1½ teaspoons vanilla

Chill a large mixing bowl and whisk in the refrigerator or freezer. In a small microwave-safe bowl, sprinkle gelatin over the cold water and let sit 1 minute or until the gelatin is absorbed. Microwave gelatin mixture on high for 30 seconds or until the mixture is clear. In the cold mixing bowl, use the cold whisk to beat the cream until peaks form. Gradually add confectioner's sugar, whisking constantly. Slowly pour in the cooled gelatin mixture, add vanilla, and mix until stiff peaks form.

NOTE: Whipped cream stabilizer, such as Dr. Oetker brand, can be found in the international section of large grocery stores or online.

Whip It

BEHIND THE SCENES at the Del, stories were constantly developing. Longtime employee Peter Zatz tells this story.

So I am working on a Saturday night, must be 1972 or so; I was fifteen years old. The manager from West called and said they were out of chocolate pies. [Only the Lake Street store had a production bakery. It supplied the other stores; calling and asking for more product was not an unusual occurrence.] I went into the walk-in cooler and found a ladder rack full of pies, but not yet topped with whipped cream or the shaved chocolate. I looked for the whipped cream to top the pies, as I had often done before, but the bowl was empty.

I went out front to find and tell Sam Weiner, the night manager. He came with me back to the bakery. Sam pulls out the recipe and puts everything into the Hobart, an industrial-size mixer. He inserts the whip, raises the bowl, and hits the "on" button. After waiting for a few minutes for the cream to whip, Sam decides it's ready and pushes the button to lower the bowl. I don't know if he thought the beater would shut off automatically when the bowl was lowered or if he forgot to turn off the mixer before he lowered the bowl, but the whip kept spinning.

You can guess what happened next. The whip continued to spin around as the bowl came down, soaking Sam and me and redecorating the bakery by splashing everything around us in flying whipped cream. I never looked at a chocolate pie the same way after that night. 𝓛

Photo by Sam Stern

Cookies and Bars

RUM PEAKS

¾ cup shortening

1 cup confectioner's sugar

1 large egg

2½ cups all-purpose flour

3 cups Butter Sponge Cake crumbs (page 113)

1 cup Chocolate Frosting (page 133)

1 tablespoon rum flavoring

2 tablespoons pecan pieces, optional

2–3 tablespoons raspberry jam

4 cups (2 pounds) chocolate, melted

2 tablespoons Buttercream Frosting (page 124)

YIELD: 12 SERVINGS

A favorite feature in our pastry cases, loved by young and old.

Preheat oven to 350 degrees. In bowl of stand mixer, combine shortening and confectioner's sugar, blending until smooth. Add egg and mix well. Add flour and mix well on medium speed. On a lightly floured work surface, roll out dough to ¼-inch thickness, cut into 12 (2-inch) round disks, and place on parchment paper-lined baking sheets. Bake for 5 to 7 minutes or until firm. Slide disks and parchment paper onto cooling racks.

Mix crumbs, chocolate frosting, and rum flavoring until smooth. Stir in pecans (if using). Top each cooled disk with ½ teaspoon raspberry jam. Mold ½ cup of frosting-cake mixture into an ice cream cone shape, placing largest end on top of jam-topped disk. Cover cone with a coating of melted chocolate and place immediately into the freezer for 8 hours or overnight. Decorate frozen rum peaks with dots of white buttercream frosting and raspberry jam on top.

FROGS!

1 cup raspberry jam
4 cups Buttercream Frosting (page 124)
3 layers Butter Sponge Cake (1½ recipes, page 113)
4 cups (2 pounds) chocolate, melted
small white candies (for eyes)

YIELD: 12 FROGS
A favorite feature in our pastry cases, loved by young and old.

Mix together jam and frosting to create a "pink buttercream." Spread between cake layers, stacking for top, middle, and bottom. Reserve extra frosting. Wrap cake in plastic and freeze for 2 hours.

Use a round 2-inch cutter to punch 12 three-layer circles out of the frozen cake. Place a rounded mound of pink buttercream on top of each, wrap in plastic, and freeze for 1 hour. Dip frozen "frogs" into melted chocolate and set on parchment paper to thaw. Cut a "V" shape into the top and add two white candies for the eyes.

ALMOND SHORTBREAD COOKIES

YIELD: 12 COOKIES
A perfect addition to any mah-jongg gathering.

5¾ cups pastry flour, or substitute cake or
    all-purpose flour
1 cup sugar
2¼ cups (4½ sticks) salted butter, softened
¼ cup large egg whites (about 2 eggs)
2½ cups slivered raw almonds
pinch baking powder
dash almond extract

Preheat oven to 350 degrees. Line baking sheets with parchment paper. Use a stand mixer to blend ingredients thoroughly. On a parchment paper–lined work surface, roll out dough to ½-inch thickness. Cut out 12 (2x4-inch) oval cookies and place on prepared baking sheets. Bake for approximately 10 to 15 minutes, until cookies are firm.

CHOCOLATE CHIP COOKIES

½ cup shortening

⅓ cup butter, softened

1 cup granulated sugar

¼ cup packed brown sugar

2 large eggs

1 teaspoon vanilla

1¾ cups all-purpose flour

¾ teaspoon baking powder

½ teaspoon salt

1 (6-ounce) package chocolate chips

YIELD: 4–5 DOZEN COOKIES

Underbake by just a minute or two for a chewy texture. This recipe, "Lincoln Del Style," was published in the Minneapolis Star on November 1, 1978.

Preheat oven to 375 degrees. Mix shortening, butter, sugars, eggs, and vanilla thoroughly. Stir together flour, baking powder, and salt. Stir dry ingredients into butter mixture. Mix in chocolate chips. Drop by rounded teaspoons 2 inches apart on ungreased baking sheets. Bake 8 to 10 minutes or until golden brown.

COCONUT MACAROONS

2 cups egg whites (about 12 large eggs)

½ cup honey or inverted sugar

1½ teaspoons vanilla

10 cups (approximately two 14-ounce bags) lightly packed sweetened flaked coconut

1 cup confectioner's sugar

½ cup all-purpose flour

2 cups semisweet chocolate chips

YIELD: 24 LARGE MACAROONS

These sweet treats are a favorite of Jack Held, one of our eager taste testers. In fact, this recipe is the one Wendi's Colorado relatives request the most. Here ya go, Jack and Howard Zelkin!

Preheat oven to 375 degrees. Line baking sheets with parchment paper. In a large bowl, combine egg whites, honey, and vanilla. Blend until stiff. Slowly fold in coconut,

⇒

confectioner's sugar, and flour. Shape mixture into 24 mounds and place on prepared sheets. Bake for 15 to 25 minutes, until slightly golden. Set aside to cool. Melt chocolate chips. Dip tops of macaroons in melted chocolate and place on a cooling rack set on parchment paper to catch the chocolate drips.

RUGELACH

16 tablespoons (2 sticks) butter, softened

1 (8-ounce) package cream cheese, softened

2 cups all-purpose flour

¾ cup packed brown sugar, divided

3 teaspoons cinnamon

1 cup golden raisins

½ cup sweetened flaked coconut

1 cup chopped nuts

YIELD: 80 COOKIES
This recipe was inspired by Tess and Morrie's longtime neighbor, Dr. Harold Berris.

In bowl of stand mixer, combine butter, cream cheese, flour, and ¼ cup brown sugar. Blend on medium speed until well mixed. Form dough into 4 balls, wrap in plastic, and refrigerate for 8 hours or overnight. Allow dough to warm to room temperature, approximately 2 to 3 hours.

Preheat oven to 350 degrees. Line baking sheets with parchment paper. Stir together remaining ½ cup brown sugar, cinnamon, raisins, coconut, and nuts.

On a floured or nonstick work surface, roll out each dough ball to a ¼-inch-thick circle. Spread one-quarter of the filling over each circle. Cut each circle into 4 quadrants and then each quadrant into 5 (1-inch) "pie wedge" triangles. Roll each slice from the wide edge into the center. Place rugelach 1 inch apart on prepared sheets. Bake for 20 to 25 minutes, being careful not to overbake.

SUGAR COOKIES

1 cup shortening (see note)

3 large eggs

1 cup packed brown sugar

1 cup granulated sugar

1 tablespoon plus 1 teaspoon baking powder

1 teaspoon salt

2 teaspoons vanilla

3 cups flour

YIELD: 4 DOZEN COOKIES

This recipe was the basis for holiday cookies in all shapes: Jewish stars, dreidels, Christmas trees, Snoopys, and more.

Preheat oven to 375 degrees. Line baking sheets with parchment paper. In bowl of stand mixer, combine shortening, eggs, sugars, baking powder, salt, and vanilla, blending on medium speed. Fold in flour. Roll out dough to ¼-inch thickness on a floured surface to use cookie cutters or portion dough into golf ball–size balls, place on prepared baking sheets, and flatten to ¼-inch thickness. Bake for 12 to 15 minutes, until slightly golden.

NOTE: Butter can be used instead of shortening, but the cookies will spread a bit when baked.

CHOCOLATE CHIP PEANUT BUTTER BARS

8 tablespoons (1 stick) salted butter,
  softened
1 cup creamy peanut butter
½ cup granulated sugar
½ cup packed brown sugar
1 teaspoon baking powder
¾ cup corn syrup
5 large eggs
½ teaspoon vanilla
1½ cups pastry flour, or substitute cake or
  all-purpose flour
1½ cups chocolate chips
melted chocolate for dipping

YIELD: 24 BARS
Cousins have offered cherished belongings in exchange for this recipe, the very first tested for this book. Wendi's college roommate, the brilliant Joanne Levine, requested these with each of Wendi's pilgrimages home.

Preheat oven to 350 degrees. Grease a 9x13-inch pan. In bowl of stand mixer, combine butter, peanut butter, sugars, and baking powder, beating on medium speed for 4 minutes. Add corn syrup, eggs, and vanilla, beating on medium speed for 2 minutes. Add flour and mix on low speed for 2 minutes. Fold in chocolate chips. Pour batter into prepared pan. Bake for 20 minutes, until golden brown. Cool bars, then cut into squares and dip edges in chocolate

CHOCOLATE BROWNIES

YIELD: 12 BARS
You cannot eat just one!

½ cup shortening
8 tablespoons (1 stick) butter, softened
2½ cups sugar
¾ cup unsweetened cocoa powder
½ teaspoon salt
½ teaspoon vanilla
5 large eggs

½ cup honey

2¾ cups cake flour

1 cup walnuts or pecans, optional

Chocolate Frosting (recipe follows)

Preheat oven to 350 degrees. Grease a 9x13-inch pan. In bowl of stand mixer, combine shortening, butter, sugar, cocoa, salt, and vanilla. Blend on medium speed for 4 minutes. Add eggs and honey and blend on medium speed for 2 minutes, scraping sides of the bowl as needed. Add flour and blend on medium speed for 2 minutes. Stir in nuts (if using). Spread batter into prepared pan. Bake for 20 minutes. Cool brownies and then spread with Chocolate Frosting.

CHOCOLATE FROSTING

YIELD: ABOUT 1½ CUPS

⅓ cup butter, softened

⅓ cup unsweetened cocoa powder

2 tablespoons honey

1 teaspoon vanilla

2¼ cups confectioner's sugar

3 tablespoons heavy cream

In bowl of stand mixer, combine butter, cocoa, honey, and vanilla. Mix well. Gradually add confectioner's sugar and cream, blending until smooth.

Breads and Rolls

LINCOLN BAKERY BREAD MAKING PHILOSOPHY

Lincoln Bakery bread is made using an "old country" process without preservatives. The method is not quick but instead is meant to achieve the best flavor. All doughs are to be rested for up to 1½ hours after mixing to get a big rise. Proof temperature is best at 100 degrees. Always cover the dough while rising to prevent crusting. After the first proof, the dough is kneaded again and set to proof until it doubles in size. The optimum dough temperature is 80 degrees. After the second rise it can be garnished as desired and then baked.

Fermentation time will vary based on home temperature, humidity, and elevation or proofing oven settings. Water amounts also vary due to the strength of the protein in the flour.

Lincoln Bakery Sour Recipe

½ cup rye or whole wheat flour

¼ cup warm water

⅛ teaspoon active dry yeast

Mix flour, water, and yeast until dissolved. Let stand at room temperature for 8 to 12 hours.

THE BAGEL *Blitz*

THE FIRST LANDLORD for Lincoln Del West was Baker Properties, which maintained close relations with the Del. Over time, the property was sold to MEPC Properties, a real estate holding company in London. To maximize revenue from the various buildings surrounding the Del, MEPC began renting to high-density tenants, which had a seriously unfortunate impact on the (lease-guaranteed) parking reserved for Lincoln Del customers. As the number of employees and visitors in the office buildings grew, Del patrons began to complain about the parking problem. In 1986 Danny Berenberg turned to MEPC and asked for solutions; the Del's lease was clear on the parking spaces allotted, and these were regularly being encroached upon. The response from MEPC was "So, sue us."

A lawsuit seemed impractical under the circumstances; it would likely take years to get the matter resolved through the court system. Danny turned to public relations expert Dave Mona to find a workable alternative. After much discussion, Dave introduced Danny to Paul Maccabee, then a junior associate of Dave's firm.

Maccabee came up with a unique idea. He printed tags that appeared to be parking citations but instead contained an appeal to MEPC Corporation to "Let My People Park." Each tag included the MEPC national headquarters' mailing address in Dallas on the reverse side. Danny and Paul produced 25,000 tags, each signed by a Lincoln Del customer over a period of weeks, and the tags were tied to individual bagels. They mailed the bagels (otherwise unwrapped) through the US Post Office, which got into the swing of the campaign and sent out a brand-new truck and uniformed crew to collect the tagged bagels for mailing—a great photo op for the local news.

Danny flew to Dallas to be at MEPC headquarters with a camera crew when the bagels were delivered. Rather than accept the bagels with a positive spirit, MEPC stationed armed guards, with actual shotguns, at their headquarters to prevent any "trespass." Danny and crew waited in front of the headquarters for several hours as the press gathered for the standoff. Eventually, MEPC sent out a spokesperson. She said, "We're sorry that you wouldn't take those bagels and give them to a homeless shelter or a food shelf," and Danny replied, "We've provided for that; we have a place that will take them immediately." Representatives were patiently waiting in the Texas sun to deliver the bagels to food shelters across the city.

The next exchange with the MEPC spokesperson made headlines in the *Dallas Morning News*. Danny told her, "I'm just here to deliver the bagels. I don't see any problem. But isn't anybody going to come out and greet us? I mean, the *Dallas News* is here." And she just looked at Danny, and he said, "There's something I don't understand. I'm from Minnesota, and we don't send our womenfolk out to do our fights." And the news crew got that, and she just sputtered, and Danny said,

"Don't you have any men in there who will stand up to me?" That was it. They published it: "Texas is embarrassed by MEPC." Of course Danny's remark would be unacceptably sexist today, but at the time it was pretty funny.

MEPC folded the very next day and came to an acceptable compromise on the parking guaranteed to the Del—without suit. The "Let My People Park" campaign won the International Association of Business Brokers and Consultants (IABBC) award for crisis communication that year, and Mona, Meyer, and McGrath (and Danny) were in London to receive it. ℒ

Let my People PARK

Join the Lincoln Del Bagel Blitz!

The Lincoln Del needs your help.

Help in convincing our landlord, Texas developer M.E.P.C., that the Lincoln Del West should not be squeezed out of existence.

Bring the parking ticket

bound into this issue to any Lincoln Del before September 7. Sign it. And walk away with a free bagel. Plus the chance to win a complimentary bagel-a-day for the next year.

It's the Lincoln Del Bagel Blitz.

Because when Minnesotans roll together, who knows what might develop?

WEST
5201 Wayzata Blvd.
St. Louis Park, Minn. 55416
Phone 544-3616

SOUTH
4401 West 80th Street
Bloomington, Minn. 55437
Phone 831-0780

EGG BAGELS

5 cups all-purpose flour, divided

1 packet (2¼ teaspoons) active dry yeast

¼ cup sugar

¼ cup oil

1 tablespoon salt

2 large eggs, well beaten

1 drop yellow food coloring

YIELD: 24 BAGELS

Morrie Berenberg once said of his success, "You concentrate on your best item—for me it's the bagel—and you do it well." This recipe, "Lincoln Del Style," was published in the Minneapolis Star on November 1, 1978.

In large bowl of stand mixer, combine 1½ cups flour, yeast, sugar, oil, and salt. Turn on hot tap water and allow to run until too hot for your hand to stand. Run water a few seconds longer, then measure 1½ cups. Add water to dry ingredients a little at a time, mixing thoroughly every time.

Use medium speed to beat dough 2 minutes, scraping bowl occasionally. Add eggs and ½ cup flour to dough. Beat at high speed 2 minutes. Turn off beaters once or twice and scrape bowl. Stir in food coloring to definite yellow color. Stir in as much remaining flour as necessary to make a soft dough that does not stick to your fingers.

Turn out dough onto lightly floured board. Knead 8 to 10 minutes, until smooth and elastic. Place dough in ungreased bowl. Cover and allow to rise 30 minutes in warm, draft-free place. Punch dough down—dough will not have doubled in bulk; turn onto lightly floured board. Using a rolling pin, roll dough into a 12x10-inch rectangle. Cut into 24 equal strips 1 inch wide by 5 inches long. Form each strip into a circle, pinching ends lightly together. Arrange on oiled baking sheets.

Preheat oven to 400 degrees. Pour water to 3½-inch depth in large heavy skillet. Bring to a boil. Starting with bagels shaped first, drop bagels into boiling water and cook 30 seconds; retrieve with slotted spoon. Replace bagels on the baking sheets and bake 15 minutes, until crisp. Cool on wire racks. If desired, baked bagels can be brushed with egg white wash made by mixing 1 egg white with 1 teaspoon water.

KAISER ROLLS

3¾ cups bread flour

1½ tablespoons sugar

1¼ teaspoons salt

1 packet (2¼ teaspoons) instant or rapid-rise yeast

1 cup warm water (110–115 degrees)

3 tablespoons canola oil or seasoned oil

1 large egg plus 1 large egg yolk

⅓ cup poppy seeds and/or sesame seeds

YIELD: 6 ROLLS
So good, we named a race after them (see page 140).

Preheat oven to 200 degrees. In a stand mixer fitted with dough hook, combine flour, sugar, salt, yeast, water, oil, and 1 whole egg. Blend at low speed for 1 minute, then medium speed 6 to 8 minutes, until dough pulls away from sides of bowl. Turn dough onto a lightly floured surface and knead gently until elastic and fully developed, approximately 5 minutes. Place dough in greased bowl and cover with plastic wrap. Proof in oven until the dough doubles in size and reaches 80 degrees (use an instant-read thermometer).

Knead the dough gently, then divide into 6 apple-size balls and place on a greased baking sheet. Press the tops of the balls to flatten a bit and indent with a Kaiser roll stamp (see note). Proof the rolls, covered, in the oven until they double in size and reach 80 degrees.

Remove rolls from oven and increase oven temperature to 400 degrees. Mix egg yolk well. Turn rolls upside down, re-stamp, brush with egg yolk, and sprinkle with poppy seeds or sesame seeds or both. Bake for 15 to 16 minutes.

NOTE: A kaiser roll stamp is available at specialty cooking stores.

THE Kaiser Roll

DANNY BERENBERG ADMITS that the Kaiser Roll race started because he and public relations expert Dave Mona, who founded the firm Mona, McGrath and Gavin (which was later acquired by Weber Shandwick and became Weber Shandwick Minneapolis), were both working too hard, and they conspired to come up with some summer activity they could have fun with *and* get away with.

Former Kaiser Roll race director Scott Schneider says that, in the early 1980s, at the beginning of the running boom, "You could put a chalk mark on the street and draw a thousand runners."

Danny and Dave, who began his career with beat coverage of the Twins and spent thirty-two years hosting the *Sports Huddle* radio show with Sid Hartman on WCCO-AM, decided to sponsor a road race in Minnesota. The United Nations had declared 1981 as the International Year of Disabled Persons, celebrating "full participation and equality," i.e., the right of persons with disabilities to take part fully in the life and development of their societies, enjoy living conditions equal to those of other citizens, and have an equal share in improved conditions resulting from socio-economic development. Other objectives included increasing public awareness, understanding, and acceptance of persons who are disabled. The UN determined that the image of persons with disabilities depends to an important extent on social attitudes, which were at the time a barrier to full participation and equality in society.

The New York City Marathon—which had begun in 1970 and had by 1981 become one of the preeminent long-distance annual races in the United States— refused to allow participation by wheelchair racers; in fact, organizers went to court to keep them

The Kaiser Roll 'It's not your ordinary race...'

I've been associated with many races — from marathons to weekend "fun runs." I've participated in them, organized them, and watched them. So last year, when I was approached to help organize a new race in Bloomington, Minnesota, I thought it would be, by and large, like most other first-year races.

I was wrong. This race, which came to be known as the Kaiser Roll, was a very special event. It provided all of the race-related details generally associated with the well-organized, longer-established races including computer-assisted timing, printed race-day programs, well-trained aid station and finish line attendants, and on-location emergency medical facilities. It also had a festival-like atmosphere with live bands, a calliope, a hot air balloon, clowns, babysitting and balloons for children and a delayed broadcast over a local television station.

Yet, another reason for the unusual success of last year's race was the attention given to a very special group of people who, until the Kaiser Roll, had not received proper regard — wheelchair athletes. Last year's race featured what many believe to be the **largest and finest collection of world-class wheelers ever assembled in a 10-kilometer race.** Among those included were **Sharon Limpert** of Minneapolis, the 1980 winner of the Women's wheelchair division of the Boston Marathon; **Jim Knaub** of Long Beach, Calif., who was the overall winner of the 1981 Boston Marathon; **Candace Cable** of Las Vegas, Nev., the 1981 and 1982 winner of the Boston Marathon's women's wheelchair division; **John Brewer** of Salt Lake City, Utah, who was the first person to complete an ultra-marathon (50 miles) in a wheelchair; and **Phil Carpenter** and **George Murray**, who in 1981 completed a 3,442 mile cross-country journey from Los Angeles to New York in their wheelchairs.

We expect most all of last year's racers to return for the second annual race. In fact, most have written to us saying that they are encouraging other wheelers to participate. In addition, officials from the charitable organizations benefiting from the proceeds of last year's race vowed to bring "bus loads" of people confined to wheelchairs to

the next race, if not to participate, at least to witness the courage and determination of those wheelers who are in the race.

But for those of you who are able-bodied runners, **don't think that the Kaiser Roll is only for wheelchair athletes.** The majority of last year's 2,000 race participants were able-bodied runners and we hope to build up those numbers this year. Estimates for the number of 1983 Kaiser Roll participants call for at least twice that of last year's. And who knows what the future may bring. We do know that our aim is to make the Kaiser Roll the top 10-kilometer race for wheelers in North America and certainly one of the featured races for all able-bodied runners in the midwest.

After only one year, the Kaiser Roll has already been added to the **Corporate Running Series** and has been named an official **event of the Minneapolis Aquatennial.** And, in addition to the family-related features of last year's race, the 1983 Kaiser Roll will include shuttle buses, race photography, a silent auction, and **ribbons to the first 10 finishers in every category.**

Prior to last year's Kaiser Roll, I felt as though it was just another race. This year, I am both proud and excited to act as Race Director for the second annual Kaiser Roll. It is a credit to the Minnesota racing community as well as to this year's three charitable recipients. I urge all of you to attend on July 16th. If you are a runner, participate. If you're not, come and cheer. Either way, you'll not forget it. But then again, it's not your ordinary race.

Steve Hoag

Steve Hoag
Race Director

An owner of GBS Sports, Inc., Hoag is a former All-American track star and captain of the cross country team at the University of Minnesota and has competed in the Boston Marathon on three occasions finishing 13th, 6th and 2nd.

out of the race. They argued that wheelchairs are dangerous to other racers, people could get hurt, and they didn't want to take the risk. (The New York Marathon introduced an official wheelchair and handcycle division in 2000.)

So naturally, Danny and Dave said, "Well, here's an opportunity; we'll include wheelchair racers." And they did. They invited wheelchair racers and runners who were blind or deaf to participate in the race, and thanks to Dave the publicity was enormous, so the Kaiser Roll skyrocketed; it got big almost immediately.

According to Danny, the first year, the able-bodied said, "Well, this is not fair; they're in wheelchairs. You've got to give them a little head start." Danny thought that was reasonable; "But of course these wheelchair racers are magnificent athletes, and they just blew the runners out of the water." The second year, the able-bodied were saying, "Well, that's not fair: they're on wheels!" There was always that tension there.

Danny says, "We had a very good time with the Kaiser Roll, but my father suspected that we were doing it just to get out of work. He was right, partly. That was not the focus he wanted on his business, so we went through all these machinations to get him interested; we had him start the race, and we had a pistol made for him, and at the moment he was doing all these things and getting all this good publicity and the adoration from the crowd, he liked it, but about two days later he was back on me, saying, 'We're not doing this again; it's too expensive.' But that was the beginning of wheelchair athletics in the country, and it led to wheelchair racers being included and recognized—that started right here in Minnesota. It was really the first major race that made wheelchair racing and blind racing heads-up with able-bodied racing, and then it got into the Olympics, and it's become an acknowledged sport. The wheelchair racers were all amateur at that time; they were just glad to be part of it. But by the end of the Kaiser Roll, they got prize money. [They] became professional athletes, just like everybody else."

"The people of Bloomington were unbelievable."

Sharon Limpert
2nd Place, Women's 5K Wheelchair Division, 1982 Kaiser Roll

ENTRY

Advance registration is $5, with early registration closing Tuesday, July 12. The race will be limited to 5,000 participants so early registration is recommended. Registration on the day of the race, if available, will be $10. Checks, made payable to The Kaiser Roll Foundation, should be sent with the detached entry form to the address indicated on the bottom of the form. All participants will receive Kaiser Roll T-shirts.

WARNING - Register early to avoid disappointment.

SERVICES

In an effort to make your race day festivities hastle-free, The Kaiser Roll Foundation has attempted to provide as many pre- and post-race services as possible. Among those services planned are:

- baby-sitting
- parking attendants
- shuttle buses
- photography
- race-day registration
- free post-race refreshments for race participants
- printed race-day programs

ENTERTAINMENT

The Kaiser Roll is more than just a road race. It is a family event, featuring a carnival-like atmosphere designed as much for the spectators as it is for the participants. Included in this year's race are:

- live bands
- balloons for children
- hot air balloons
- refreshments
- a calliope
- clowns
- cotton candy
- delayed television broadcast

THE RACE

The Kaiser Roll is made up of two separate races. The 5 kilometer race will begin promptly at 8:30 a.m. while the 10 kilometer event will begin at approximately 9:30 a.m. Due to the anticipated crowds, be sure to allow plenty of time for parking and warming up.

Every effort has been made to make the Kaiser Roll as well organized and as well staffed as possible. The Foundation, along with the Race Director, has surveyed many other races throughout the country and has combined the best ideas into this year's race. From the time the starting gun goes off until the walk down and away from the finishing chute, trained Kaiser Roll personnel will treat all participants with respect and care. Also, remember that the Kaiser Roll is included in this year's Corporate Running Series and has been named an official event of the Minneapolis Aquatennial. Among the other features associated with the race will be:

- computer recorded timing
- digital time readouts
- aid stations with water & ERG
- on-location emergency medical facilities and personnel

POST-RACE EVENTS

Having completed a race, it can be quite anti-climactic to simply walk to your car and drive home. Instead, the Kaiser Roll will feature post-race festivities that will allow runners to visit with each other, listen to bands and compare times. In addition, a post-race ceremony will include:

- merchandise awards to winners of all categories
- ribbons to the first 10 winners of each category
- conclusion of silent auction

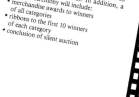

CONTINUED NEXT PAGE

THE Kaiser Roll

CONTINUED FROM PREVIOUS PAGE

According to a *Star Tribune* article by Annie Breitenbucher published on July 7, 2000,

> In its glory years the Kaiser Roll attracted as many as 6,000 runners and raised as much as $81,000 for charity. But, first and foremost, it was a premier event for wheelchair racers.
>
> Race founder Danny Berenberg, former chief executive officer of the Lincoln Del restaurants, saw to that. Having overcome polio as a child, and observing his father's struggles while [using a wheelchair] because of a stroke, Berenberg wanted to organize a race that centered on wheelchair athletes.
>
> "It was a race for wheelchair athletes first and runners second," said Tami Oothoudt, an elite wheeler from Stillwater. "It felt like that was the way it was marketed."
>
> More than marketing, prize and expense money paid to wheelers demonstrated the race's commitment to the sport, and to attracting a world-class field. Three times in its history the Kaiser Roll was designated the national wheelchair championship race at 8K and 10K distances. In 1986 it was host to the world 10K wheelchair championships.

Danny says, "Those early years were just a lot of fun, and the Kaiser Roll became really famous. I'm very proud of that. It was the beginning of heads-up racing athletics, proving that wheelchair athletes can beat you. One year they wanted the wheelchair athletes to start behind, and I said, 'I'll do that, but you'll be sorry. They will run you down. They'll hurt you.' Wheelchair racers are very competitive, as much so as any major athlete."

Lee Snyder of On-Demand Productions remembers, "[Danny] gave me a press pass to photograph the Kaiser Roll, and I was hooked. I produced a three-minute slideshow (three projectors, big stereo sound, original music), and Danny used it at every fundraiser he could sponsor. I won an award for photography; wheelers gained an Olympic event. My favorite button at the Kaiser Roll was given out by Quickie Wheelchairs: 'Nothing beats a Quickie!'"

ONION PLETZELS

YIELD: 6–8 SERVINGS

Thank you, Jon Tarshish, for reaching into your Northside Bakery/ Malinsky roots to test these marvels. Your directions are perfect!

olive or vegetable oil

1 onion, coarsely chopped

½ cup warm water (110–115 degrees)

1 teaspoon sugar

1 packet (2¼ teaspoons) active dry yeast

4 cups bread flour

1 teaspoon kosher salt

1 large egg

1½ teaspoons poppy seeds

In a large skillet, warm 1 tablespoon oil over medium heat and cook onions until translucent and slightly caramelized. Set aside. In a small bowl, combine warm water with sugar and yeast. Let sit until foamy, about 10 minutes. In a large bowl, stir together a scant cup water, 1 teaspoon oil, flour, salt, and yeast mixture. Knead dough until fully developed with an elastic texture, about 8 to 10 minutes. Place dough in a large, lightly oiled bowl, cover with plastic wrap or a damp cloth towel, and allow to rise in a warm room for 1½ hours or until dough doubles in size and reaches 80 degrees (use an instant-read thermometer).

Preheat oven to 350 degrees. Line 2 baking sheets with parchment paper. Divide the dough into 2 equally sized balls and punch a cavity in the middle of each. Place balls on prepared baking sheets and fill cavities with onion mixture. Let dough stand for 10 to 15 minutes.

Whisk egg and stir in poppy seeds. Brush egg wash on entire roll. Bake for 11 to 12 minutes.

CARAWAY RYE BREAD

SOUR STARTER

1 cup rye flour

½ cup water, room temperature

⅛ teaspoon instant or rapid-rise yeast

Mix ingredients together and let stand at room temperature in a loosely covered container for at least 12 hours prior to use.

YIELD: 1 LOAF

Many thanks to Steve Wiesner for perfecting this challenging recipe for home use. Yeast is introduced twice: once for the sour and once for the dough. The resulting taste is simply the best.

If you won't be using the starter right away, it may be refrigerated for up to a week before feeding. To feed, allow to reach room temperature. Mix in 1 cup bread flour and ½ cup water. Allow to stand at room temperature at least 8 hours before returning to the refrigerator. Do not store in a tightly sealed container. Be sure to feed it weekly.

To use a prepared starter, bring it to room temperature before proceeding. Always feed the starter before returning it to the refrigerator.

SPONGE

1 cup bread flour

1 cup rye flour

1¼ cups water

¼ teaspoon instant or rapid-rise yeast

In a mixer fitted with the paddle attachment, combine flours with water and yeast. Mix for 5 minutes or until smooth. Allow sponge to stand, covered, at room temperature, for at least 4 hours, overnight if possible.

DOUGH

1½ cups bread flour

2 tablespoons caraway seeds

1 teaspoon salt

½ cup warm water (110–115 degrees)

1 tablespoon vegetable oil

¼ teaspoon instant or rapid-rise yeast
2 tablespoons sour starter (see left)

Stir together flour, caraway seeds, and salt. Set aside. In bowl of stand mixer fitted with the dough hook, combine the sponge, water, oil, yeast, and sour starter. Mix on low speed to combine. With the mixer running on low, add dry ingredients in thirds, scraping the sides of the bowl as needed. Mix for 5 minutes. Cover and let stand 20 minutes. Mix on medium speed for 10 minutes or turn out dough onto a lightly floured surface and knead for 10 minutes. The dough should be tacky but not sticky (see note). If the dough is sticky, add flour. If kneading with the mixer, the dough may curl up around itself on the hook: stop the mixer occasionally to push it back down. Place the dough in a lightly oiled bowl, cover with plastic wrap, and allow to rise at least 3 hours, until almost doubled in size. Gently scrape the dough onto a lightly floured surface, being careful not to deflate.

Form dough into a loaf, place on a parchment paper–lined baking sheet, and allow to proof for at least 2 hours or until doubled in size. (Alternatively, refrigerate the dough overnight, allow it to come to room temperature for at least 4 hours, and then form the loaf and let proof.) Thirty minutes prior to baking, place a heavy sheet pan on the bottom rack of the oven. If using a baking stone, place it on the center rack. Preheat oven to 400 degrees. When the bread has doubled, score the top with a sharp knife or razor and transfer baking sheet to the center rack of the oven or place loaf directly onto the preheated baking stone.

To create a crisp crust, immediately pour ½ cup water onto the sheet pan and close the oven door, taking care not to get scalded by the steam. After 3 minutes, add another ½ cup water to the bottom pan. Reduce the oven temperature to 350 degrees and bake for 45 to 60 minutes, until the internal temperature of the loaf is 200 degrees. Remove the loaf from the oven and allow to cool for at least 2 hours before slicing.

NOTE: Sticky means the dough sticks to your fingers, spatula, etc. Tacky dough will stick but then release and leave your fingers/spatula pretty clean.

PUMPERNICKEL BREAD

½ teaspoon instant or rapid-rise yeast

1 cup warm water (110–115 degrees)

1 teaspoon salt

3 tablespoons canola oil

3–4 drops caramel or brown food coloring

3½ cups pumpernickel flour

Preheat oven to 200 degrees. Dust 1 (8½ x 4½-inch) loaf pan with flour. In bowl of stand mixer, combine yeast and water, mix on medium speed, then add salt, oil, food coloring, and flour. Mix for 6 minutes, until dough pulls away from the sides of the bowl.

Knead dough by hand until elastic, about 10 minutes. Place in ovensafe bowl and cover. Proof in preheated oven until dough doubles in size, about 1½ to 2 hours; dough should reach 80 degrees (use an instant-read thermometer). Knead dough for 2 minutes after the first rise and keep as one loaf or split into two. Place in prepared loaf pan(s), cover, and proof a second time, until dough doubles in size. Increase oven temperature to 375 degrees. Bake for 45 minutes.

YIELD: 1 LOAF

Pumpernickel bread is notoriously complicated to make. Personal flavor decisions abound: Plain rye flour? Pumpernickel flour? Molasses as a coloring agent? Or food coloring? How easy is it to find pumpernickel flour, anyway? (Answer: Bob's Red Mill sells it, and we also found it at Amazon.com.)

CHALLAH

3 cups bread flour or other high-gluten flour

¼ cup sugar

3 teaspoons instant or rapid-rise yeast

1 teaspoon salt

3½ tablespoons hot water

4 tablespoons (½ stick) butter, softened

2 large eggs, room temperature

cornmeal

sesame or poppy seeds, optional

YIELD: 1 BRAIDED LOAF

Be creative: add chocolate chunks, cinnamon sugar, raisins, figs, and more to the mixture before kneading. How about peanut butter and jelly?

In bowl of stand mixer, combine flour, sugar, yeast, salt, and water, blending on low speed. Add butter and 1 egg and mix on medium speed for 4 minutes. Let dough stand, covered, in a warm place for 1½ hours to rise; dough should reach 80 degrees (use an instant-read thermometer). On a lightly floured surface, knead the dough. Divide into 3 portions, roll each into a 12-inch rope, and then braid ropes together. Set in a warm place, ideally a proofing oven, to rise for 1 hour.

Preheat oven to 350 degrees. Line a baking sheet with parchment paper and sprinkle with cornmeal. Beat remaining egg and mix in 2 tablespoons warm water (110–115 degrees). Set challah on prepared pan, brush the egg wash on the top, and sprinkle with sesame or poppy seeds (if using). Bake for 20 minutes or until golden brown.

PAN TWIST BREAD

YIELD: 1 LOAF
A customer favorite and
a regular pantry item.

3 cups bread flour

¾ teaspoon salt

¾ teaspoon sugar

¾ teaspoon instant or rapid-rise yeast

2 large eggs

6 tablespoons oil

1½ cups water

sesame or poppy seeds, optional

In bowl of stand mixer, combine flour, salt, sugar, yeast, eggs, oil, and water and blend for 5 to 6 minutes. Let dough stand, covered, in a warm place, preferably a 200-degree proofing oven, until dough reaches 80 degrees (use an instant-read thermometer). Rest dough at room temperature for 1½ hours, covered. Separate dough into three pieces and braid. Place in an 8½ x 4½-inch loaf pan. Set in a warm place to rise until doubled in size.

Preheat oven to 375 degrees. Sprinkle top of dough with sesame or poppy seeds (if using). Bake for 45 minutes, until golden brown.

WHOLE WHEAT BREAD

3½ cups whole wheat flour

3 tablespoons powdered milk

1 packet (2¼ teaspoons) instant or rapid-rise yeast

1 teaspoon salt

1½ tablespoons sugar

1½ tablespoons malt syrup (see note)

1 tablespoon oil

½ tablespoon honey

1¾ cups water

YIELD: 2 LOAVES

We debuted this bread ahead of many other bakeries, who followed suit during the "health craze" of the seventies.

In bowl of stand mixer, combine all ingredients and blend on low speed for 1 minute, then on medium speed for 7 to 8 minutes, until well mixed. Proof dough, covered, in a warm place or a 200-degree proofing oven until dough reaches 80 degrees (use an instant-read thermometer). Rest dough at room temperature for 1½ hours. Line 2 (8½ x 4½-inch) loaf pans with parchment paper. Divide dough into 2 loaves and place in prepared pans. Cover and proof again until dough doubles in size.

Preheat oven to 375 degrees. Bake for 45 minutes or until golden brown.

NOTE: Malt syrup, like Eden's Barley Malt Syrup, is sold at co-ops. The amount of water is approximate. Depending on the absorption of the flour, you may need more or less.

Holiday

KITKA

3¾ cups bread flour

3 tablespoons sugar

1 packet (2¼ teaspoons) instant or rapid-rise yeast

2¼ teaspoons salt

¾ cup water

¼ cup oil

2 large eggs

¾ cup golden raisins

YIELD: 1 LOAF

Raisin or plain, this turban-shaped bread filled the front bakery racks every Rosh Hashanah, the Jewish New Year.

In bowl of stand mixer, combine flour, sugar, yeast, salt, water, oil, and eggs. Blend at medium speed for about 5 minutes, until elastic dough forms. Add raisins and mix well. Proof dough, covered, in 200-degree oven for 1½ hours or until dough reaches 80 degrees (use an instant-read thermometer).

To make this turban-shaped challah, roll dough into a long, 2-inch-wide rope. Coil part of rope in one large circle, then continue coiling into smaller circles piled on top of each other, closing with the smallest circle at the top. Place on a parchment paper–lined baking sheet and proof in 200-degree oven for 1½ hours or until dough doubles in size. Increase oven temperature to 350 degrees. Bake for approximately 30 minutes or until golden brown.

PASSOVER SPONGE CAKE

10 large eggs, separated

1½ cups plus 1 tablespoon sugar

¼ cup orange zest

⅓ cup orange juice

1 teaspoon warm water

½ cup potato starch

½ cup matzo meal

¼ teaspoon vanilla

YIELD: 1 (10-INCH) CAKE
At home we layered this cake with Lemon Curd (page 118) and Whipped Cream (page 125).

Preheat oven to 350 degrees. Grease 1 (10-inch) angel food baking ring or line with parchment paper. In bowl of stand mixer, beat egg yolks and 1 tablespoon sugar on medium speed for 1 minute. Add orange zest and juice and water and beat on high speed until batter is light in color.

In a separate bowl, whip egg whites and remaining 1½ cups sugar until soft peaks form. Gently fold in potato starch, matzo meal, and vanilla by hand. Gently fold in the yolk mixture by hand. Pour batter into prepared pan. Bake for 30 to 35 minutes, until golden.

PASSOVER POPOVERS

¾ cup water

1 tablespoon sugar

1½ teaspoons salt

3½ tablespoons shortening

2 cups matzo cake meal

8 large eggs, separated, at room temperature

YIELD: 16 POPOVERS
Full of flavor, these are great warmed with butter.

Preheat oven to 400 degrees. Spray a popover or muffin pan with nonstick baking spray. In a large saucepan, bring water, sugar, salt, and shortening to a light boil. Remove from heat and stir in cake meal. In bowl of stand mixer, whip egg yolks at medium speed for 2 minutes. Transfer to a separate bowl and set aside. Add dough from the saucepan to the stand mixing bowl. On low speed, slowly add back the eggs, mixing for 1 minute. In a separate bowl, beat egg whites until they form peaks; fold into batter. Fill compartments of prepared pan ¾ full. Bake for 12 minutes, then reduce heat to 350 degrees and bake for an additional 15 to 20 minutes or until popovers are golden brown.

PASSOVER BAGELS

⅓ cup water
1¾ tablespoons sugar
½ teaspoon salt
4½ teaspoons shortening
1 cup plus 2 tablespoons matzo meal
7 large eggs, at room temperature

YIELD: 8 BAGELS

These bagels made some of the best sandwiches seen in the lunchrooms of many St. Louis Park public schools during the week of Passover.

Preheat oven to 400 degrees. Line a baking sheet with parchment paper. In a large saucepan, combine water, sugar, salt, and shortening and bring to a boil. Remove from heat, then stir in matzo meal. Transfer to a stand mixer and slowly add the eggs, blending until well mixed. Form the dough into bagel shapes and place on prepared baking sheet. Bake until slightly browned, about 12 to 18 minutes, depending on the size of the bagel.

POUND CAKE, FILLED POUND CAKE, OR HOLIDAY FRUIT CAKE

POUND CAKE

2 cups (4 sticks) butter, softened

2¼ cups sugar

1 tablespoon vanilla

1 teaspoon lemon zest, optional

6 large eggs

1½ teaspoons salt

5 teaspoons powdered milk

4½ cups flour, sifted

FOR FILLED POUND CAKE

2 tablespoons butter, softened

⅔ cup sugar

4 teaspoons cinnamon

FOR FRUIT CAKE

1 cup chopped candied red cherries

1 cup chopped candied green cherries

1 cup finely chopped pecans

YIELD: 2 FILLED CAKES OR 3 FRUIT CAKES
A delight to serve and eat. A customer favorite any time of day.

Preheat oven to 325 degrees. Grease 2 or 3 (8½ x 4½-inch) loaf pans and line bottoms with parchment paper. For filled cake, mix together filling ingredients and set aside. For fruit cake, toss cherries and nuts in 1 cup flour for pound cake and set aside. In bowl of stand mixer, blend butter on medium speed until light and fluffy. Gradually add sugar, mixing well. Blend in vanilla and lemon zest (if using), then add eggs one at a time. Blend in salt and powdered milk and then add flour 1 cup at a time, blending well. For fruitcake, gently fold in floured cherries and nuts. For plain cake or fruit cake, divide batter among prepared pans. For filled cake, layer batter with filling. Bake for 45 minutes to 1 hour. Cool on a wire rack for at least 10 minutes before turning out of the pan.

POTATO KNISHES

This home version includes a method for making the dough. Or take the easy route and use store-bought phyllo dough.

YIELD: 8 KNISHES
The original knish recipe from Del prep kitchen notes: Grind potatoes on nut chopper. Hand mix potatoes plus one hand full of schmaltz made of chicken fat cooked with onion.

½ cup schmaltz, plus more for glaze
1 large onion, chopped
8 large potatoes, peeled and chopped
4 large eggs plus 1 large egg yolk
vegetable oil
1 teaspoon baking powder
½ teaspoon salt
approximately 1⅔ cups (250 grams) all-purpose flour
butter, melted

In a large skillet, warm schmaltz over medium heat, then add onion and potatoes and cook until soft. Mash together and add salt and pepper to taste. Set aside.

For dough, in a medium bowl beat 2 eggs with 2 tablespoons oil, baking powder, and salt. Gradually add the flour—just enough to make a soft dough that is no longer sticky—mixing with a fork to begin with, then working by hand. Knead dough for about 10 minutes, until very smooth and elastic, sprinkling in a little more flour if necessary. Coat with oil by pouring a little into the bowl and turning the dough around in it. Cover the bowl with plastic wrap and set aside for an hour.

Preheat oven to 350 degrees. Line a baking sheet with parchment paper. Beat 2 eggs in a small bowl. In a separate bowl, stir together egg yolk and 1 teaspoon water. On a well-floured surface, roll dough into a very thin 8x16-inch sheet and brush with melted butter. Cut into 8 (4-inch) squares. Add filling to the middle of each square. Brush inside edges with whole egg wash, pull sides together on top of filling, and press to seal. Brush top with egg-and-water wash or schmaltz and set on prepared baking sheet. Bake for approximately 30 to 40 minutes, until golden brown.

PARTY *Trays*

MANY OF THE WOMEN IN THE FAMILY—Baubie Tess, her daughter Penne, nick-named Mickey; Mickey's daughters Wendi (this book's author) and Tammi; Morrie's sisters Ann, Agnes, and Gloria; Gloria's daughters Sorah and Carri; and oftentimes head prep cook Edna Dye—gathered in the kitchen at the West Del to make the popular meat trays for holiday parties and celebrations. Starting in November and working all the way through January, they spent many days rolling the various meats tightly on top of a display of cheeses garnished with parsley and pickles and the tasty centerpiece of chicken, tuna, egg, or salmon salad.

Those on the deli tray assembly line sat for hours, gossiping about everyone and everything as Tess walked around to inspect their work. Was the salami rolled tightly enough not to unroll? Was the cheese displayed correctly? Don't skimp on the potato salad! Was there ham in this order? What about the corned beef? Was it lean enough? Try this chopped liver: enough schmaltz? ⌞

ACKNOWLEDGMENTS

SPECIAL THANKS TO

my mom, Penne Gail Berenberg, Keeper of the Secrets, for all things
about our family and the Del
and my husband, Rick Rosenstein, for his love, boundless energy,
and support

AND TO

Danny Berenberg

Jena and Jake Berenberg

Traci Bransford at Stinson Leonard

Dana Casher

Thomas L. Friedman

Dara Moskowitz Grumdahl

Laurie Harper at AuthorBiz

Daniel Hemiadan

Mark Jones at Vongsouvan Fine Arts

Sam and Sylvia Kaplan

Malie and Mary McDevitt Kraljic

Paul Maccabee

Dave Mona

Drs. Rick and Arlene Noodleman

Jill Osvog

Sheldon Rhodes

Brett Rosenstein

Matthew Rosenstein

Dr. Scott M. Sokol

Sam Stern

Gale "Stormy" Strommer

Rollie Troup

Millie Wiesner

Sam Wiesner

Steve Wiesner

Tammi Zelkin Wiesner

Karin Winegar

Sue Zelickson

Jack Zelkin

Jaimie Zelkin

June Zelkin

Rabbi Marcia Zimmerman

THANKS ALSO TO

Jeanne Anderson at the St. Louis
Park Historical Society

Mike Bell

Dick Bernard

Dr. Harold Berris

Dr. Stuart Borken

Kate O'Brien Bronson

Scott Coleman

Cecilia Sutton Dobrin

Steve Dobrin

Joan Donatelle at Lunds & Byerlys

Brett Dorrian

Elaine Fries

Robin Melemed Gale

David Garber

Nancy and Jack Held

Susie Held

Rhonda Teich Hickey

Patti Isaacs

Bill Johnson

Jack and Doll Laboe

Joanne Levine

Merle Minda

Merrick Morlan

Deborah Morse-Kahn

Barbara Mraz

Barbara Pratt

Michelle Price

Carmen Rubio

Liz Herstein Salsberg

Paula Lichter Shapiro

Anna Simon

Vicki Katzovitz Siskin

Kelly Swartz

Adam Tarshish

Cindy Tarshish

Evan Tarshish

Dr. Gabriel and Mariya Tarshish

Jon Tarshish

Julie Tarshish

Dan Wallace

Audrey Wilcox

Alaine Swerdlick Wilensky

Peter Zatz

Many thanks to all who contacted us to share their incredible stories about the Lincoln Del. We read more than three hundred emails over the last few years and feel humbled and lucky to have received such heartfelt memories. Everything about the Del is extraordinary, especially our loyal customers and employees.

ABOUT THE AUTHORS

Wendi Zelkin Rosenstein

was born in Colorado and raised in St. Louis Park in her family's business, the Lincoln Del. Her grandparents Tess ("Baubie") and Moishe ("Zadie") Berenberg spoiled her from babyhood with bakery, deli, and restaurant treats. She learned how to make kreplach at age seven, participated in the opening of the third location, Lincoln Del South, as a "soda jerk" at age eleven, and waited on customers behind the deli counters of Lincoln Del East and West throughout high school. She perfected the art of bottling schmaltz by the time she was twelve. At Berenberg family dinners, she contributed her two cents on developing many of the recipes that originated in her Baubie Tess's kitchen and subsequently found their way to Lincoln Del menus.

Wendi inherited her Baubie's talent in the kitchen and still makes (and teaches cooking classes about) all traditional Lincoln Del dishes. On her Baubie and Zadie's insistence she did punch out at the Del to attend Brandeis University, graduating with a BA in politics in 1984 and then a JD from William Mitchell College of Law in 1987, hence her proud liberal bohemian tendencies and a fervent love of a good cause and a colorful argument.

She and her husband, Rick, are proud parents to their identical twin sons who share her love of travel. You can often find her soaking up women's travel stories and planning her next adventure.

Bowing to years of nagging from relatives, friends, and strangers, she is proud to bring these recipes to the many loyal customers who still sing the praises of the Lincoln Del as a favorite Minnesota culinary institution.

Anne Kittridge Naylor (Kit)

is a professional writer and an amateur chef. "My mother was a resentful cook," she remembers, "and no wonder—for most of her married life she had to come up with dinner for six every night of the week. Her go-to meal was creamed tuna on toast. If feeling particularly festive, she'd throw in a fistful of frozen peas for color. I realized I was a foodie when, at age twelve or so, I could taste the difference between a proper white sauce—that actually made the dish relatively palatable—and canned cream of mushroom soup, which I now regard as a crime against nature."

The eldest of four children in a career Air Force family that moved every couple of years (*"every* year all through junior high . . ."), Kit grew up feeling rootless, longing for the sort of community she might have found at the Lincoln Del. She has transformed her hunger for belonging into Algonquin Hotdish—a monthly gathering/salon for Twin Cities creatives, i.e., writers, artists, graphic designers, photographers, and assorted other freelancers. Kit and friends founded this group in 2004, and she has led the organization ever since. She earned a BA from Carleton College in Northfield, Minnesota, and takes post-graduate classes at the Loft and the Iowa Writers' Workshop.

WITH THANKS TO

Judy Datesman, culinary arts guru since our college days; to Linda Fisher, Kristin Henning, and Nancy Naylor McCullum, because I'm always happiest when perched at their kitchen counters; to Becky Palmer and Lloyd Zimmerman, who rave about every dish I make for them; and to journalist Karin Winegar, who, when Wendi first approached her about collaborating on this project, replied, "Oh, no, I'm not a cook, but I know someone who *is*."

— A K N —

RECIPE INDEX

SUBJECT INDEX